W
N

WITHDRAWN

THIS IS
OUR CHINA

© *Wide World Photos, Inc.*

The two leaders of China on the grounds of their home in Hankow.

This Is Our China

By

May-ling Soong Chiang
(Madame Chiang Kai-shek)

HARPER & BROTHERS PUBLISHERS
New York and London

CONTENTS

[5]

[6]

Acknowledgment is made to the editors of *The Forum and Century*, *Asia*, New York *Herald Tribune*, *North China Daily News*, *Shanghai Evening Post*, and *Birmingham (England) Post* for permission to reproduce articles from some of their issues.

Section 1

WHAT CHINA IS THINKING TODAY

I.

CHINA'S PRESENT, PAST, AND FUTURE

"We must develop our resources with the definite object of co-operating with international producers and consumers."

WHEREVER the Japanese have been they have marked our land with ruin. They have left scars upon our earth, our hearts, and our minds—indelible scars—scars which never can be healed or eradicated. I wonder if the Japanese people realize that? They should begin to do so quickly if they ever hope to recover any semblance of prestige, or even standing, in China—or in the world, for that matter. The myriad ghosts they have made will take a lot of laying—ghosts of men, women, and children; of ancient cities, towns, and villages; of workshops and factories; of the little shops—the places of handicraft of the millions. You never saw such monstrous criminality. Yet at this allegedly advanced period of civilization there is no law and no nation or nations to check or punish the criminal; no applicable international instrument of any kind available.

So far we, in China, have not had much opportunity

to achieve any particular modernized national greatness. We have been having too much warfare since 1911 to have had the time to become even an acceptably passable republic. Perhaps we have been too content, in a way, to live upon the musty reputation of our ancient glory, with — as caustic critics may well describe them—intramural intellects pretending to competency in the handling of modern systems and devices. I have to say "intramural" because we are too big a country to be called provincial — and, also, we have a wall. Whatever we are, we have to admit that we found it difficult for many years to march fast toward national success, though we really had girded our loins, and had started, full of hope, when our progress was stopped by the aggression of the Japanese.

Our dilatoriness to date has really been largely due to the fact that our national characteristics never have been given a proper airing, or scrubbing, or dry cleaning; never have been pegged out on the line, so to speak. But there is one thing that I am devoutly hopeful about, and that is that the terror and the death and the burning that have been unceasingly inflicted upon us since July 7, 1937, will not have been in vain so far as a readjustment of both our national outlook and our international attitude is concerned. Were it all to be in vain it would be just as ghastly a catastrophe, in a way, as the one we are now enduring.

I have expressed the hope that we would tread the

democratic path, but must mention that, while the desire to adhere to the democracies is pretty widespread and substantial at the moment, there is a school of thought developing which is asking with some impatience, but also with some pertinence: "What have the governments of the democracies done for us?"

That is, from their point of view, a natural and justified question. One has to admit that the governments of the democracies have done nothing tangible or practical, not even to protect their own interests. They fear, of course, that if they become too articulate just at present they may find themselves put in the position of having to defend their words with guns. Naturally, they do not want war, but if it has to come, they want to be ready for it.

While that attitude of mind is perfectly understandable, a large section of our thinking people cannot comprehend why the democratic governments still fear to express themselves in practical terms to Japan on the question of her infamies and inhumanities. After all, we seem to have been left frigidly alone by every democracy to fight as best as we can, with our inadequate equipment, for the principles which the democracies espouse—the sacredness of treaties and international laws, and all that —as well as for our own salvation. One disconcerting thing is that, though we have been deserted, as it were, the democracies seem to be willing to listen with a strange-

[15]

ly attentive ear to the demands of Japan that the powers should remain neutral. Japan, with the air of a grievously injured innocent, is crying for help to destroy us as if it were her country that was being wrongly invaded and consumed by fire, and her people who were being blown to fragments by the guns of Chinese aggressors.

Those of our people who question the advisability of our keeping in with the democracies point out that it is the amazing studied neutrality of the democracies that enables Japan without any restraint to continue killing our people, violating our women, and making a wilderness of all of our territory that she has been able to penetrate.

I feel convinced that our nation, if it pulls through this catastrophic war, will change in many ways. I may be deluded, but I think I see hopeful signs of appreciation in the awakened mind of some, at least, of our leading people, of the value of sustained effort born of co-operation and of national unity.

It has taken China a long time to unify, a short time to show the strength and advantage of that unity. Hitherto, fear of Japan produced a sort of paralysis among us. Not a weakness peculiar to China, be it said, for fear has done that to other countries too. But now that it has been proved in our civil and social arenas, no less than on our battlefields, that even the alleged invincibility of the Japanese can be countered with some success by concerted effort, we may expect that the intelligent among our people will hereafter be ashamed not to show good citizenship and energy and honesty in the forwarding of constructive and helpful reforms. If they do not—if too many of them are sluggards—I foresee the rise of forces that will be dangerous for them. The old apathy will never again be tolerated. China is bound to shed her worn-out gowns of indifference and laziness—celestially characteristic though they once may have been. The awakened minds of the present generation and the developing ones of the next will see to that.

In my estimation one of the most interesting discoveries made in China during recent months is that factional issues can be subordinated to national interests and be forgotten when there is a will to do so. How large those issues have always loomed in our national lives! How insurmountable they have always seemed! Yet, they can, when the occasion comes, disappear with uncanny completeness.

Another significant thing that is happening, and perhaps the most important thing, is that our country is surely finding its soul. We will have a tremendous social and political problem on our hands as soon as time for rehabilitation comes, no matter who wins. Perhaps our surest sheet anchor will be this new spirit that is developing; a spirit that will, in time, mature on a nation-wide scale. There is an obvious need for spiritual solace. I think our people are realizing where it can be found. Some know; many are groping. I notice a certain amount of what might be described as awareness of supernatural influence working on our behalf. Also, there is suppressed awe—awe at our nation being able to last as long as it has done in the face of what was believed, when the invasion began, would be certain defeat and probably extinction within a few months. People are wondering whence came our unexpected strength. Out of the quiet and calm acceptance of belief in that strength is springing a spirit of heartening and sturdy confidence. In some prominent quarters there is a sense of acknowledgment of unworthiness to take a real part in such a great national struggle. There is quite a bit of soul-searching too. If that will but spread, if a humility will come to us that will bite into the self-assertive know-allness that used to characterize many of us, it will be a forceful influence for permanent progress and good.

We, in China, need substantial and unashamed humility. We also need to see a change of heart in large numbers of the officially prominent, as well as in leaders in civilian circles. Especially do we need it in those who have hitherto been, perhaps unconsciously, obstructionists to national progress by virtue of their failure to co-operate in forwarding different lines of public endeavor. The present poignant, national suffering; the ever-present prox-

imity and sight of crashing, instantaneous death; the vast-
ness and awful suddenness of destruction by far-flung explosives all these have had a noticeable effect in sobering
innumerable people, and bringing them to earth, as it
were.

*   *   *

If I judge aright, as I have said, humility is also showing itself in various places. All I hope is that we can
capitalize it. It may help, among other things, to subdue
the thoughtless ones who think that national economic
advancement can be acquired without special qualifications on the part of our people, and without the assistance
or co-operation of the outside world. That is a fallacy.
Somehow many of us never seem to have got over the
ideas of our forebears who believed that they could live
their lives within the confines of our borders, self-
contained and immune from outside influences—a stupid-
ity that should have been demolished one hundred years
ago, or at least fifty years ago.

It has been the manifestation of a spirit of intolerance
of foreign methods, oftentimes to the detriment of foreign
commercial interests, that makes foreign investors,
merchants, politicians, and economists suspicious of us,
and skeptical. One can hardly blame them. After all, commerce is mutually advantageous; should be reciprocal in

its benefits. Of course, the Chinese attitude arises from the fear of the aggressiveness of foreigners.

Then, too, there is the old scorn of foreign technical help. Many of our fellow countrymen, who, I happen to know, have previously discounted the value of foreign technical experts and, by obstructing the experts, have prevented our country from deriving the full benefit of foreign knowledge and experience, have now learned from this unequal war why we have had to suffer so much for so long from our inadequacies. They have previously always proceeded along their misguided recalcitrant way oblivious of possible reactions. It is, of course, too late now for their penitence to cancel the consequences of their follies, but in the mere realization that China has lost in numerous ways by not absorbing all that was available to her from the advisers and experts—engaged by her at high expense, may it be said—there is hope for a wisely practical attitude of mind in the future.

That this war and its calamities will provide the impetus for important reforms is certain. With the realistic changes that are inevitable in responsible quarters progress is sure to be more rapid, more realistic, and more endurable once we can get a chance to settle down to the work of rehabilitation. At any rate, there will be so much to do and so little money with which to do it that we will be compelled to put a curb not only upon amateurish experimentation, but also upon incompetents, if we wish to improve. Always we have been cursed with incompetents, and with persons of inordinate conceit.

If ever China really needed applied wisdom it is now, and will be in the future. We therefore have to see to it that only capable and positive-minded people are put in charge of nationally important constructive work. The fools have had their day with their little follies. Or, I hope they have. And, incidentally, in their day they contrived to bring upon us quite an abundance of scorn, if not loss, which is neither a cheerful reflection nor a nice thing to have to admit. But I, for one, hate to try to hide truth from myself, and I am far too intellectually honest to try to hide it from others under some all too obvious kind of camouflage.

One thing I am surely hoping to see is a practically wise policy for economic development. It has always seemed to me a tragic crime that there has been so much shortsightedness in our reluctance to enlarge our economic possibilities. We managed to contrive a definite political line of thought and advancement, but we have been surprisingly dilatory—or delinquent—about opening up our natural resources and finding more avenues of employment for our masses through a scientific and systematic program of economic expansion. A wise, concerted effort to raise the standard of living of our people has not been persistently pursued, though it has been much talked about.

*　　*　　*

Mere talk has always been another of our banes, which reminds me of a story (perhaps, with a moral) of Kwei-chow province. In that remote region there lived a Tiger, but never any other quadruped of any size, until someone imported a Donkey. One day the Tiger met the Donkey; was startled by its size and formidable appearance; sat back on its haunches and soliloquized. "Is this threatening-looking stranger going to conquer me?" he mused, as he meticulously surveyed the armament of the Donkey. "By golly, he has four hard rocks on the ends of his legs; he has a big head, full of great teeth. And, I ask you, just look at those ears." The Tiger crept slowly around the Donkey. "By gum," said Old Stripes, "I must be careful. He may be as dangerous as he looks—I'll find out." The Donkey grazed quietly, as donkeys do. The Tiger crept about as silently as tigers creep. He studied the Donkey's rear end, gave a quick nip at his fetlocks. A heehaw, a squeal, a fast-flying pair of heels — and back the Donkey went to his grazing. "So that's that," quoth the Tiger, with a sigh of relief, "I'll try the front side." He pondered as the Donkey's strong array of teeth bit at the grass. Then he deftly nipped the Donkey's long ear. The

Donkey brayed, squealed in panic, swiftly pivoted, lashed the atmosphere with his heels, and settled down once again to the job of feeding. "Ah, ha," laughed the Tiger, stroking his whiskers, and licking his chops, "you can only talk; you are not half as dangerous as you look; you can only squeal and kick; you are — why, bless me! You're one of those pacifists. Dang it, I'll eat you." And he did.

*   *   *

There was a beginning, however, to solve the economic problem. We were hopeful that through the People's Economic Reconstruction Movement we would start to move the age-old mountains of lethargy and really get somewhere. Before we could really get going, however, the Japanese started to move against us. They were apprehensive lest our other reforms mature, and probably saw that success was about to invest us with more than empty blessings.

The last thing the Japanese wanted was an organized, prosperous China. They wanted China, of course, but they themselves wanted to do any organizing that had to be done so that they could control its direction and capture the possible profits for their own benefit. They strove for years to keep us in chaos; then they brought war to us and, with it, they are sedulously bringing material ruin. No doubt by this time they are amazed at what they have done, for they are ruining themselves, have forged a shackle of debt for armaments about the neck of the terrified nations, and, incidentally, have sown about the world, as Cadmus sowed in his furrow, swarms of dragon's teeth. I wonder what the harvest will be?

*   *   *

Sometime ago I wrote somewhere that out of the evil being wrought against us good may come. How I pray for that. I think, as I have said, that our country will surely find its soul in the trying torment in which we are involved. If we do, we shall be able, without difficulty, to go about the business of upbuilding our country upon new lines. In any case, one thing we should insist upon is that there shall be no more experimentation with political or economic theories and nostrums. We surely should have had enough of that by now. There is no more time for it. Above all, we will have to be eminently practical — even ruthlessly so.

*   *   *

We have also to inspire the advanced nations with confidence in us and in our intentions. I have said that I thought the democracies were probably afraid that ill would come to them if we came out of the war victorious. If that feeling exists it is as unfortunate as it is curiously shortsighted. Recently the Generalissimo drew a remark something like that from a foreign visitor. He promptly quashed the idea with the statement that it would take China thirty or fifty years to rehabilitate herself after this war, and a hundred years would pass before she would be able to compete with anyone, even if such a thing would ever be possible. On the other hand, he added, foreign products, especially machinery, tools, and manufactured articles of all kinds, would be in heavy demand for many decades, and foreign investments would be a constant necessity. Foreign countries may well be alarmed if Japan is permitted to conquer China. Then there would be reason for tears. Japan would swamp the world with cheap goods of all kinds, and buy virtually nothing in return.

We are faced with the immediate necessity of providing our broken people with the means of livelihood; we must give our commercial men scope; above all, we must try not to do that at the expense of vested interests belonging to other nationals. We must prove that we have no intention of doing so.

Foreign trade must go on. Its expansion is to China's direct benefit. It should be encouraged in every way because we have great needs, and, in time, we will have raw materials to satisfy the needs of others. Investments must be protected.

* * *

I have hopes that a planned economy will be adopted—something eminently practicable and tangible which will give our people a dignified and unequivocal opportunity to achieve something worth while for their personal respect and their prosperity, as well as for their national dignity and well-being.

I should like to see village industry carefully developed wherever it is possible for raw materials to be produced and worked up to supply the daily needs of the people. There will have to be mechanical aid in some cases; but I hope that machinery never will be brought to China to save labor as its first principle and requirement. Machinery should be used to make necessities which hands cannot make, but there it should stop. Nor should cutthroat competition in manufacture be permitted. In that the workmen suffer.

I am against labor's being sweated for the benefit of the conscienceless plutocrats. I am against its being sweated in any circumstance. We have so much scope in so many directions to help our people help themselves that we would be worse than stupid to burden them with trials and tribulations bred of strikes and other menaces to peace such as are attendant upon industrialization as it has developed in outside countries.

*　　　*　　　*

If we emerge safely from the calamities of this war, one brake will be put upon us that should have a restraining influence upon development of too many large industries. That is the brake of exhausted finance. It will not be easy to plunge into great schemes of factory development, and that, to my mind, is a good thing.

There is so much to be done by hand, so many hands to do it, that wisdom dictates energetic arrangement of opportunities and possibilities for manual work just as quickly as circumstances will allow. I am trusting that the awakening which has come to everyone as a result of this war will be responsible for close consideration of these things in order that we shall, with certainty, put our feet securely upon the highway to peaceful prosperity.

If we, in China, are given the perception to promote co-operative effort with foreign experts and capital, there is nothing to stop our growing up into a strong and capable nation: self-respecting, and gaining the respect of all peoples who have so far marched ahead of us in national development. At all events, we are lucky in one thing: we have for our guidance and profit the precious advantage of the experiences they have gone through. That is something mere money cannot buy. If we fail to use it we shall deserve all the condemnation that can be visited upon us, and all the scorn. I am hoping that the psychological changes which this warfare is sure to effect will include the elimination of that old folly of ours which allowed us to play at industrialization, at such great cost, oblivious of the wisdom of using modern methods in accordance with modern practices and experiences. Well, most of our factories have now been sacrificed, so we can start afresh.

*   *   *

I find myself wondering quite a lot whether out of this restarting (whenever the chance for that will come) we may not be able to contribute something definite to the solution of the problem of world economy. The whole world is on the verge of war because it is alleged that there is too much "hogging" of raw material. Of course, when Japan forces war upon us on the alleged ground that we would not co-operate with her she said something grotesque that must insult world intelligence. Everyone knows that Japan was able to get anything from us on her own terms. She got all of our iron ore—I said all—at incredibly low prices; she got all our pig iron, until the Hanyehping

smelters at Tayeh went out of business, at the absurd price
of $3 (Chinese currency) per ton, which is equivalent to
$1 United States currency; she got all the soya beans she
could buy at low prices (her nationals controlled the business, in a sense), and she had the general market for other
things in the palm of her hands. She made war not because she wanted co-operation, but because she wanted
economic domination through administrative control. She
wants China as a base for a Japanese continental empire.
When her statesmen reiterate that they have no territorial
designs on China they are guilty of mendacity unworthy
of those controlling a first-class power. They made similar
protestations when they were busy occupying Manchuria
—and what is Manchuria now? Manchuria is under Japanese control garbed in alleged imperial trappings as a
puppet empire.

But there is, I feel, no possibility of a similar fate over-
taking the rest of China. So we can proceed to consider the
development of our resources when the time comes (it
may be a long time) with the definite object of co-
operating with international producers and consumers.
We have a barter agreement with Germany that was working satisfactorily until Japan stepped in and dislocated
communications; there is no reason why we should not
have others—or have some systematic plan for the promo-
tion of the sale of raw products and the scientific develop-

[29]

ment of natural resources so that all buyers should have an equal opportunity to meet their needs.

If world troubles are primarily due to lack of raw materials, then let us open up the necessary avenues to allow the world to buy of our supplies upon a mutually advantageous basis, with a fair field to all and no favor for anyone. Of course, that would not suit Japan, who is a monopolist; nor would it suit those in our own country who, for diverse reasons, some questionable, favor monopolies instead of open competition. But what of that?

*　　*　　*

Proper machinery should be set up for all national purchases. I am strong for a waterproof and airtight purchasing organization which would see to it that all suppliers and tenderers are equitably treated, have an honest run for their money, and are fully protected from sharp practice and from any unscrupulous officials who may survive the dragnet of some sort of purge which will be inevitable. I am strong for life imprisonment, at least, for rogues and vagabonds who masquerade as conscientious officials.

The one thing that we should insist upon in the new and difficult time ahead of us is the establishment of a civil service, properly paid and pensioned. We will have some tradition to live up to now, as a result of the fighting, so we might just as well create traditions in civil life that will, in time, make for our national solidarity and security. Cleansing Augean stables is neither a pleasant nor an elegant pastime — but we have to clean them. A lot has been accomplished already, and the New Life Movement is turning out to be quite a potential instrument in this regard.

*   *   *

I see in the New Life Movement much wider scope for national and public good than was anticipated when it was conceived. I wonder if you know what the scope of that movement really is? Many do not. There is, or used to be, an idea abroad in foreign lands that it is something for the officious policeman or boy scout to amuse himself with to the aggravation of the harmless pedestrian who does not have his coat buttoned up or who has the corner of his mouth festooned with a cigarette.

It can, however, stand the comedy, or the satire, or the ridicule, so effective and substantial is its worth, so far-reaching its influence. That is why general reforms are possible through its agency. We believe, as Mencius believed, that "the people are the most important element in the nation." He ranked the sovereign third, after the spirits of the land and grain.

[31]

After all, the New Life Movement begins at the beginning of things connected with the life of the people. It
is concerned with the houses in which they dwell, the
food they eat, the clothes they wear, their comings and
goings in society. You may call that materialism; I call
it common sense. Our people are great home lovers, fastid-
ious about their food and what they drink, careful in the
preparation of clothing appropriate for the seasons. They
are, in fact, the most socially conscious race in the world.

Lest all the benefits of life be enjoyed by a small mi-
nority, and the great multitudes of toilers remain unsatis-
fied, the New Life Movement has appeared as a great
Chinese champion of the people's right to the best that
their country can provide.

Hammered out on the anvil of experience are four car-
dinal principles of life, as we Chinese understand life:

1. The way in which human beings behave one toward
   another.
2. Justice for all classes within our social framework.
3. Honesty in public administration and in business.
4. Self-respect, and a profound sense of the value of
   personality.

Four ancient characters, *Li, I, Lien, Chih,* cover those
accumulated values. To all our people they are pillars upon

which our civilization rests. By following these fundamental principles we find that we can remold the life of our people.

*   *   *

One can scarcely omit mention of an important development here that promises to be of great moment in the future — that is the growing influence of our women. There was a day when women in our country were not encouraged either to exhibit themselves to the public eye or to make their presence felt in public affairs. They have lived through, or down, that man-made restriction. They have emerged from the stern cloister of the home; they are now exerting considerable weight and displaying appreciative intelligence in social service. That will increase as time goes on.

In the operation of their side of the New Life Movement they have major opportunities and responsibilities. They are acquitting themselves with tremendous credit; they show an unexpected adaptability and capacity for achievement. Furthermore, they are eager and anxious to do what they can. Especially at this time of national crisis is this noticeable. They are working all over the country —working with the hospital problems, with relief work of all kinds, with the care of the war orphans, twenty thousand of whom we are collecting for immediate up-bringing, and so on.

There is immense scope for the influence of women in the future regeneration and rehabilitation of our country. In fact, the land will be laid so waste wherever the Japanese troops go that the immediate work of looking after the suffering survivors, which is peculiarly a woman's task, will be onerous, exacting, and exhausting.

When we are going to get the chance to resume work on a nationwide scale it is hard to tell. Japan is assaulting us now with all her accumulated might, exerting herself to the utmost to try to subjugate us. I see our country being swept by fire and swamped in blood. We cannot help it. Japan has taken pages out of the history of the barbarians. She is applying them, embellished with refinements that make savagery and infamy sublime. It was Genghis Khan who established and upheld the doctrine of death to defeated populations in order to prevent suppressed hatred bursting out in time to his undoing. Whole populations went to death under the swords, the arrows, and the knives of his hordes. He swept like a torture through the heart of China.

Hot on his old tracks the Japanese are now attempting to follow. With newfangled engines of war they have reduced his primitive methods of massacre and his fiery holocausts to a science. They have gone further. They have

outshone him in the subjugation of survivors by introducing a new finesse. They bestow "rewards." In addition to
any food or pay that may be granted them at the end of
the day, laborers in Japanese employ are given bonuses in
the shape of narcotic injections. To salve the agonies of
the impoverished, or the sufferings of others who find
themselves unconsolable under the benign control of the
Japanese, opium and its derivatives are peddled everywhere, and facilities are provided for the weak and demor-
alized to secure drugs and so find surcease from their mental and physical tortures. History has proved that Genghis
Khan, with all his annihilating cruelties, failed to subjugate us. What prophecy can be made regarding the results
of the sinisterly advanced methods of the Japanese?

We can do no more to protect our country and people
than we are doing. We are fighting as well as we know
how, with inadequate equipment. But we will not give up.
All I hope is that we shall be able to get the necessities for
our armies until peace comes. If we cannot get those necessities, it will be because the democracies decline to help
us get them.

If democratic governments have not, as is alleged, forgotten their principles, and have not abandoned their responsibilities under treaties and international law, surely
a conscientious sense of justice will, before it is too late,
inspire them to do the right thing by China and her people

who have been in process of immolation since July 7,
1937. That is all we ask — that the right thing be done
by us who are victims of belief in treaties, and who re-
fused to abandon the League of Nations and the Democracies when we could have done so.

* * *

Running true to form we, in China, are preparing for
peace while the Occidental nations are preparing for war.
It is said that the Chinese always do things contrary to
the Occidental habit of mind and custom. We read a book
backwards; we write a line downwards, vertically instead
of horizontally, starting on the right side and ending on
the left side of the paper; we shake hands with ourselves;
and so on. So why should we not prepare for peace when
other nations are arming themselves for war? We want
peace, and we need it; but it must not be peace at any
price. It will have to be peace with honor. If it is not, then
the world will be in a grievous situation, for it will mean
that brute force and barbarism have signally triumphed
over civilization—for we will be in ruins and, *ipso facto,*
all we fought for and stood for will be in ruins. That "all"
embraces civilization.

While we are fighting, however, we are looking ahead,
because we are unafraid. In our classics the wisdom of

such a policy is applauded. Confucius once said to an inquirer: "If a man takes no thought about what is distant, he will find sorrow near at hand." We are trying to avoid the sorrow which usually characterizes the aftermath of war. We will be faced with more poignant grief and suffering than usually overtake countries that have been burned out by war, but we are trying to meet them by preparing now. We are systematizing contacts for the lost ones, especially children; working out the problem of locating survivors and then locating their lands; planning for relief and for employment in the work of rehabilitation. We hope that we will have an effective organization to avoid calamities attendant upon the demoralization of millions of homeless and impoverished people. We are working hard to solve that problem.

We hope, too, that we will be able to invoke the help of that age-old system of ours that has hitherto kept our people together in the worst of political upheavals — the clan organizations and the patriarchal family system. In every prominent village, town and city, there were, until the Japanese came, ancestral halls where were kept the records of the families of the clan. Here, too, and in various temples, were stored lists of deeds of land or property which had been given at the death of one or other well-to-do member of the clan as endowments for the benefit of one clan or another. These endowments took the form of a piece of land here, of a parcel of land there, a stand of timber, or some other productive property. The land was usually let for farming, fifty per cent of the value of the crop or proceeds going to the endowment fund.

Through ages past these endowments have benefited the poor, permitting them to live and secure education; or have contributed to the preparation of aspirants for government office secured through the famous old examination system which took candidates to different provincial capitals where they sat for days in narrow cells until they had completed their papers. These examinations led to the hall of fame in classical accomplishments or to a position in the official class which then administered the country. A member of a clan in high office was always a form of insurance for the clan in times of natural calamity, so official rank for one or more members of a clan was a much-prized possession. If anything is left of the records of this system in the regions occupied by the Japanese they will assist us in getting our refugees back to their feet, and in continuing without interruption the course of our agelong civilization.

*　　*　　*

Militarily, we have sustained ourselves and we will continue sustaining ourselves. The invaders, by virtue of their tremendous weight in equipment, may win battles, but they will be compelled to stick to the ruts of long lines of penetration, while we, if we have munitions, can move about our country like pieces are moved about the squares of a chessboard until we checkmate Japan and win the war.

I have received many letters from friends in America urging me to go there to assist in the raising of funds for our sufferers. Unhappily I cannot be in two places at the one time, and since America is renowned for its un-bounded generosity and its virile reaction to suffering and injustice, I am inclined to believe that it is more important for me to stay and help here. American people will give just what they want to give, whether I visit the country or not. If they decide that the terrible wholesale butchery and burning and outraging that is being perpetrated by Japanese soldiers upon the Chinese people does not war-rant their aid, then they will not give it; if many of them feel unmoved by the threat of catastrophe to the world if Japan defeats us, then nothing I can say will affect them one way or the other. If they know that we are fighting the battle of civilization against a revival of barbarism, while defending our heritage, and still do not wish to contribute to any relief fund, nothing I could do would change their hearts or minds.

I wonder if I am to be convinced by Aldous Huxley's *Ends and Means* that the spirit of charity is subsiding in

America? Huxley quotes Dr. R. R. Marett as saying that "real progress" (we were brought up to believe America to be the most progressive country in the world) "is progress in charity, all other advances being secondary thereto." Huxley himself says: "Periods of advance in charity have alternated with periods of regression. . . . The present age is still humanitarian in spots; but where major political issues are concerned, it has witnessed a definite regression in charity. . . . Technological advance is rapid. But without progress in charity, technological advance is useless. Indeed, it is worse than useless. Technological progress has merely provided us with more efficient means for going backwards."

I cannot believe that the American people wish me to appear as Exhibit A, or to act as a sort of before-dinner cocktail to sharpen the appetite and add verve and zest to the "jollying" of dollars out of their pockets and purses. I am no conjurer; and I am no cocktail. I am just a simple-minded human being who refuses to believe that the America I knew and loved has descended to that level. My friends must be mistaken. I want to go to America, but the work to be done here to help save our country and our soul necessitates, as in a storm at sea, all hands being on deck through all the watches. Here is my place, and here I must stay until relief comes in the shape of a change in the state of this war, which will give us superiority over the invading enemy or bring us defeat. Then I may go to America to see my friends and to make new ones. When I do go I wish them not to regard me as one coming with ulterior motives, but as one coming back to old scenes and old friends because I have wished once more to enjoy them. I should like people to feel that my visit was undertaken because it would be of interest to them and to me, and because I want to learn from the American people, and because they wish to impart, things which it would be useful for me and my country to know. It would not be a material harvest that I would be seeking to garner but one of spiritual and mental stimuli. I feel sad even to hear the goodhearted America I knew being described as requiring artificial stimulation to arouse what once were its inborn charitable and humanitarian impulses. I would be horrified to have to believe that such a thing were true.

We feel deeply grateful to all in America who have spontaneously given of their best to succor our distressed people. Friends have given liberally, some lavishly, of their time and their money to help us. Our everlasting appreciation goes out to them all, as it does to the many who have prayed for us, who have expressed sympathy for us, who have worked in movements for us, who have given practical demonstration of their feelings for us, and their realization of the menacing threat to the world that this aggression in China means, by boycotting all things

Japanese. All we can give in return is a promise to try to continue the singlehanded struggle we have been engaged in, difficult and unequal as it is, for we know that if we do lose the whole world will lose, especially those nations which are now enjoying the freedom of democracy. In the fulfillment of this determination to fight on we give of our lives and our livelihood, and all we hold dear.

2.

HOW WILL WE
SAVE CIVILIZATION?

*"The very door of diplomacy seems to
have been slammed shut upon religion."*

IN 1931, without justification and without declaration of
war, the Japanese invaded Manchuria and annexed it.
They tore up treaties, used international law codes to
light the fires of barbarism, and defied democracy with
threats and with brandished weapons.

The democracies did nothing. Nor did we, at that time,
because we were counseled to have an abiding faith in the
League of Nations and in the infrangibility of treaties.
How vain our faith and our inaction proved to be, you
have reason to know. But others in the world did act.
Those who dreamed of power at any price quickly took
advantage of democratic inertia.

Their vast armies of aggression were soon ruthlessly
crushing out of existence the lives and the liberties of many
free peoples in various parts of the world. Japan also accepted new encouragement, and the tramping of her
troops and the crashing of their bombs were soon heard in

[43]

China proper, while their diabolic licentiousness was given free rein.

For more than two years now the Japanese have been venting their criminal ferocity on us. This time we depended on no one. Weak though we were to meet the formidable might of Japan, we struck back. We are still fighting and we shall continue to fight although our trust in Western civilization was rudely shocked by what looked like complete abandonment by the democracies of the treaties they had signed to guarantee human decency and to safeguard China's sovereignty and her national integrity.

Could we, left alone as we were, be blamed for feeling that, while the aggressor nations had openly challenged civilization, the democracies were quite indifferent to its fate?

What conclusion do you think we could draw from the knowledge that the great United States was supplying Japan with all the gasoline, oil, and materials she needed to enable her to continue to send her airplanes and her mechanized forces about our land to blast the lives out of our people and to raze our homes to the earth?

Yet, incongruously, it was from the government of the United States that the first ray of hope and encouragement ultimately came to us that the aggressor might be called to account.

For that hope and that sign we were deeply grateful. The recent abrogation by the United States of its commercial treaty with Japan was the first open step taken by any democracy, since aggression began, in condemnation of Japan's treachery and inhumanities. The people of China now hope that America's denunciation of criminal aggression and her avowed proscription of force as an instrument of national and international policy will not be allowed to cease there. Nor has it if the forthright warning conveyed recently to Japanese leaders in Tokyo by American Ambassador Joseph C. Grew is to be regarded as a criterion.

Oh, how I have urged all these years that some such frank warning be given the uninformed Japanese people! Oh, how we of China have looked for it and hoped for it from all the democracies!

Our stricken people can now only hope that the United States will fortify that statement of her intolerance of Japan's continued flaunting of international rights by expressing with all the solemn weight that is warranted her definite refusal to be a partner any longer to Japanese inhuman destruction of Chinese life and property.

The United States can do that by withdrawing from Japan the facilities hitherto granted her to obtain from American sources the means she has so long used with ruthless barbarity to effect that destruction.

We feel we are justified in that plea—because for America to do otherwise would be tantamount to her admission that civilization had foundered and that the gods of expediency and Mammon had been set up in the temples of men's minds and hearts to replace the real God in which America always has declared she places her trust.

The tragic calamities which now menace civilization are surely born of the appalling facility with which so many men in so many parts of the world—in order to shirk their responsibilities and trim their financial sails to the totalitarian typhoon—have been bending backwards at the shrine of expediency and Mammon, instead of bending forward in humble and contrite supplication to their hitherto acknowledged God.

Thus, the very door of diplomacy seems to have been slammed shut upon religion. Yet, religion is the main pillar of civilization and without it there can be no international righteousness, no justice, no common decency, and no guaranty of the honoring of the pledged word. There can presently be no confidence in treaties because, as we know now, treaties uninfluenced by religious scruples are violated just as soon as they become irksome to unprincipled governments which are covetous and which contemplate irregularities in seeking possession and power.

The word of men as embodied in international documents appears to be fast becoming without bond, without standing, without worth. If civilization is now to be saved, we must recover that unselfish devotion and fervor which characterized the medieval Crusaders. We must regain power and stand unflinchingly for those high principles upon which democracy was originally formed so that the liberty of men and the sanctity of human rights shall not disappear from the earth.

Without religion no state can long endure. That should now be clear enough. If religious principles governed all treaty makers, there would be no treaty breakers. If religious feeling beat in the hearts of would-be destroyers, there would be no destruction.

If religious thoughts entered the minds of those who profit from the sales of munitions to international law-breakers for subjugation of victims by aggression, there would be no aggression and there would be no victims.

We Chinese women and people are, however, victims —the original ones, in fact—of the resurrection of barbarism that has practically supplanted international treaties and codes and stained with shame this advanced period in our so-called civilization.

The very fact that this should be so is a remarkably sad commentary upon modern ideas of upholding the worth of treaties whose humanitarian safeguards supposedly were characteristic of civilization.

But when religion and all that it implies returns to inspire and govern men in all their relations with their fellows it is certain that international decency of conduct will also return. It is certain, too, that jealousies, injustices, suspicions, antagonisms, and war will quickly vanish and that right will prevail for the lasting good of humankind.

To restore peace that passeth all understanding in personal and world affairs, we women have a mighty task imposed upon us. The opportunity to do great good has been given us by this near breakdown of civilization, by this abominable prostration before the fetish of expediency, by this sight of millions of men marching to their doom, by this unparalleled orgy of selfish and wicked use of brute force to destroy humanity in a mad will-o'-the-wisp pursuit of personal power.

Throughout the ages the progress of civilization and the stability of society have been measurable by the amount of influence for good that women have exercised in their communities. It is a heritage that we women cannot ignore. It is one that we must uphold, one of which we must be worthy.

There is no standing still, no going backward. We can only go forward and we should do that in the spirit of the Crusaders with their invincible cross ever before them.

Unless a radical change comes over the hearts and the minds of men, some of us, at least, will live to see civilization perish by the very means used so long and so ruthlessly to destroy China. There is only one thing that can prevent such a disaster to humanity—it is religion; whose partial eclipse I lament.

When national consciousness and individual consciousness are developed through a belief in religion, when religion is accepted as the central pivot and motivating force of life and conduct, then the doom of civilization may be averted, but not until then.

3.

OUR DESTINY IS WITH
THE DEMOCRACIES

As SOON as the voice of the cannons dies down we must hurriedly face the task of completely reconstructing cities, towns, and villages. We even have to rebuild the nation. Bombs not only have shaken the lives out of people and buildings; they have shaken the fabric of national administration. When rebuilding does have a chance to begin, we must follow a plan that will produce a national edifice such as to make us a proud member of a peaceful family of progressive democratic nations.

To my mind, our destiny is with the democracies, because our people are inherently democratic in nature and spirit. If we survive we have the opportunity to become a great organized democracy. That is, of course, if democracy itself survives in the world.

Section II

PROGRESS IN CHINA

FINDING THE VOICE
OF CHINA

*"The most significant landmark on the
highway to progress is undoubtedly
the encouragement given to the people
to express their opinions."*

PROGRESS in China is not to be measured by any international standards. Nor can the merit or the magnitude of changes of any kind be so estimated. A realistic conception of what is happening in this ancient land can be obtained only by comparing the present [1] with the not so distant past and, at the same time, by keeping in sharp focus the details of that agelong background which has so mystified Occidental observers. It, however, constituted the real China, and upon it is based everything that goes to the making of those Chinese characteristics which, by their unfamiliar nature, amused many foreigners, puzzled most, and exasperated some who had neither the patience nor the sympathy to endeavor to understand them. But, above all, progress can best be measured by keeping constantly in mind the effects of the turbulence that ensued

[1] Written in 1936.

as a result of the revolution that brought about the overthrow of the dynastic system, and by remembering that fundamental national progress is not necessarily merely materialistic or indicated by the construction of great works, or by substituting a silent motorcar for a screeching wheelbarrow.

Revolution is no easy thing to introduce, or easy to carry through, in a land like China. Hidebound with conservatism, suspicious of all things, superstitious, mostly illiterate, and void of all conception of the responsibilities of citizenship and public service, a huge population like that of China possesses, by virtue of its very ignorance, tremendous powers of passive resistance. This can impede, and delay, and frustrate reforms that the Occidental imagines could easily be introduced if only because of their apparent practical value, the ostensible logic of them, and their obvious necessity.

However, reformers anywhere have notoriously hard lives to endure. In China they have been beset with innumerable difficulties that do not exist elsewhere. The launching of any major scheme of improvement, to say nothing of any potentially sweeping social reform, has consequently been equivalent to entering upon an endurance test, out of which come triumphant the ones having the greatest supply of patience, persistence, and philosophy, and, at times, physical strength.

PROGRESS IN CHINA

For several years following the revolution efforts were made to effect radical reforms and reorganization. In a sense some were successful, and some steps were taken that have been of lasting good. But the introduction of measures calculated to have widespread influence upon the lives and character of the people were delayed, and sometimes strangled, by reason of conditions which developed and enabled unscrupulous military officers and others to build up coolie armies, or bandit gangs, with the object of personally controlling different districts or provinces throughout the land.

There was a negation of progress in such a condition. But gradually that system has broken down. One after another the selfish and unpatriotic usurpers of power have been overcome, and a unified China has begun to emerge.

Step by step with the crushing of the selfish incompetents and the bandits in one region and another went measures to ameliorate the unhappy lot of the people, and as the latter gradually learned from experience that such measures really were for their benefit, and not for their further exploitation, they eventually applauded with surprise and relief the arrival of a new day. Newspapers, perforce, chronicled administrative and other improvements, and gradually there developed in various parts of the country that public opinion, hitherto an unknown factor in national affairs, which has so remarkably influenced the

trend of events during the last few years. In this practically unnoticed development is the most significant
sign of progress in China since the fall of the Manchu
dynasty.

Its effects and influences are even now possible of cate-
gorical record. For instance, what has become known as
the Fukien rebellion was swept away with surprising swift-
ness solely because public opinion throughout the country
was against it, and because the people of the province, of
their own volition, assisted the troops of the Central Government to drive out the unscrupulous leaders of the movement. This despite the fact that the so-called national
heroes, the leaders of the 19th Route Army, were in the
forefront of the revolt. Szechwan Province — where war
lords who fought over four hundred civil wars in twenty
years, impoverishing the richest province in China,
seemed to reign supreme—fell into line with the requirements of the Central Government so suddenly when the
time arrived that observers were quite startled.

What seemed impossible also swiftly occurred in remote Kweichow Province where the oppressive provincial
government was quickly dislodged. And, more to the
point, the early collapse of the Kwangtung militarists, in
their ill-starred attempt in conjunction with Kwangsi to
oust the Central Government, was so precipitate that observers of former events, who failed to recognize and prop-

erly appreciate recent developments throughout the country, were amazed that such things could be.

Popular opinion, born of the recognition of what the Central Government has been doing for the people, and feeling the new power of freedom of expression that has come to it, exerted itself with amazing vigor, and from all sides the leaders of this new revolt were assailed. Joining in the clamor which arose in other parts of China was also the voice of the people of Kwangtung Province itself. They have suffered so much for so many years under the tyrannical rule of officials, who were now ready to plunge the country into renewed warfare and bloodshed, that they surprised everyone by their eager welcome of Central Government control of their province. And their unexpected attitude immediately influenced several important Kwangtung army generals and the air force. Some of the former promptly announced their determination not to participate in civil war and to give adherence to the Central Government. The whole air force, moved by a like spirit, flew off at dawn one day and thus dramatically abandoned the leaders of the revolt. Those leaders incontinently fled.

Whether, of course, the reforms which the Central Government will introduce will please everyone remains to be seen.

The influence of public opinion further manifested itself upon Kwangsi provincial leaders who continued to threaten war. Some high officials fled, airplanes escaped, and some generals showed intention to mutiny. The people of the province resisted war measures, farmers were reported to have fought, and, in places, killed conscription officers. In fact, public opinion exerted itself so continuously that the leaders were left with a forlorn hope on their hands.

The Central Government, exhibiting unusual patience, waited and watched, and pleaded with the Kwangsi leaders to be wise in national interests if not in their own, so that the horrors of civil war should not be let loose upon the land, so that the people should be saved from further suffering. After a few months the leaders showed that they, like their Kwangtung colleagues, recognized the weight of popular sentiment, and accepted the terms of the Central Government, thus bringing to an end the possibility of what threatened to be one of the most tragic civil wars that ever broke out in China.

Consequently, the most significant landmark on the highway to progress is undoubtedly the encouragement given to the people to express their opinions. And if the word "progress" embraces moral as well as material betterment, then it must be acknowledged that remarkable progress has taken place in China during the past few years, for it is only within that period that the people have been able really to realize the changed nature of the administration that came in with the National Government, and the widespread character of the reforms, compatible with local conditions, which the government set under way as soon as possible.

The years immediately succeeding the successful overthrow of the Manchu dynasty were lost, in a sense, owing to the failure of the persons who contrived to assume power to realize that the liberty supposed to be conferred by a republican form of government is not license. Many likewise failed to understand that the country was not theirs to exploit for their own personal benefit, and most of them felt that they were in nowise servants of the people but the masters of them.

The expression, "Who are the people?" so much heard among old officials, which rang for aeons down the corridors of old-time yamens, is no longer audible. The old fashions and the old ideas have gone, and the people have now asserted themselves to such effect that their voice will henceforth carry weight in national discussions and in all future crises.

Perhaps it is folly to prophesy, but at least it is not idle to hope, that the period of civil war will end with elimination of the last of the factors that make insensate internecine conflicts possible. Left to themselves, the people of China, and the officials, and the army will not recklessly submit grievances, and especially personal ones, to the arbitrament of arms, but will have them dealt with in a constitutional manner as befits the dignity of a progressive state. I repeat, advisedly, if China is left to her own devices.

Next month constitutionalism is designed to come to China, and that, it is to be hoped, will mark the inauguration of definite national progress where the voice of the people will rule.[2] Any progress that has gone before has been but the foundation, but that foundation has been well and truly laid.

Upon it has been built the realization by the people of the possession of a voice and the ability to use it. That alone is sufficient to produce a moral satisfaction that surely will promote better citizenship and will develop loyalty and patriotism. For centuries the people were ruthlessly taught that an official class, to the exclusion of all others, governed China, and they were brought by bitter experi-

[2] The First Plenary Session of the Fifth Central Executive Committee of the Kuomintang, held in December, 1935, resolved that the Draft Constitution of the Republic of China should be promulgated on May 5, 1936, and that the National Assembly to decide on the date of the enforcement of the Permanent Constitution should be convened on November 12, 1936. The election of delegates to the National Assembly, however, could not be completed before October 10, 1936. By the resolution of the Standing Committee of the C. E. C. the convocation of the National Assembly was postponed and the later date, November 12, 1937, was resolved upon by the Third Plenary Session of the C. E. C. The Sino-Japanese hostilities which broke out in July, 1937, caused the convocation of the National Assembly to be further postponed.

ence to realize that if they were to save their heads they had to give up trying to save themselves and, above all, to abandon attempts to save the country from the maladministration of the official class. The consequence was that the people lost all interest in public life, in patriotism, and in the affairs of the country, and applied themselves solely to the task of protecting the interests and promoting the welfare of their families and their clans.

When the Republic came, pledged ultimately to relieve them of their woes (it will do so someday), it consequently found existing a deep and vast ignorance of the requirements of that form of government, and it has taken years — till now — to educate, even casually and cursorily, sufficient of the population to know what is required of them so that they could in some measure impart the knowledge to others. Large sections of the people seem now to have awakened, and articulation (if not profound wisdom), so long suppressed, has come to them. Nor have they been awakened by any form of desperate theoretical teaching, but by a practical demonstration of what a properly organized and supported government could do for them.

As soon as it assumed office the existing National Government began to demonstrate its intention to develop the welfare of the people by creating organs for their betterment. And it took one significant step that has, perhaps, been forgotten. As early as a few months after its establishment at Nanking in 1927 it called into being a National Economic Conference and a National Finance Conference, and they were significant, if not spectacular, inasmuch as the delegates to those conferences embraced, for the first time in Chinese history, leading bankers, industrialists, and merchants. Here was signal evidence of the *bona fides* of the government in its promises to depart radically from the old traditions that excluded the voice of the people from the councils of state, and to enlist the support of civilian brains and experience in laying the foundation of a better administration.

Among other things, too, the government called the various magistrates to a conference at Nanking and subjected them to an educative course on the proper conduct of officials toward the people. The average age of these officials was over fifty years, and they were instructed as to the rights of the people to have their grievances heard, to be protected, and to be properly considered in the administration of laws and regulations. Mainly the officials were enjoined to assist the people in the presentation of their claims and complaints, and were warned that acts calculated to be contrary to the public weal, and militating against the rights of the people, would redound to the discredit of those responsible.

Indeed, from the beginning of the Republic in 1912 patriotic minds have been bent to the task of ameliorating the lot of the people by providing them with means to raise their standard of living. Dr. Sun Yat-sen issued his industrial and railway schemes, and from time to time measures have been devised to provide for the establishment of industries to utilize raw products, even if conditions in many cases militated against satisfactory fulfillment. Political unrest did, for years, render abortive practical economic efforts, but now a definite program has been adopted which will in course of time—backed up by more enlightened public opinion — strike at the roots of economic stagnation.

This will give the investing public and the progressive industrial and mercantile leaders the encouragement, the security, and the protection necessary to ensure the long-delayed systematic development of national and industrial resources, and the scientific production of raw materials.

While it is not necessary to detail financial and other reforms that have been inaugurated, national prosperity will, conditions permitting, be statesmanlike, systematic, and sustained, and gradually there will come to China complete elimination of all those factors which have, one way or another, contributed to the stagnation that has in the past prevented her from assuming her legitimate role in international affairs. Certainly the National Government intends to pursue a policy aiming at material betterment, and the fulfillment of plans in that direction will benefit not only China and her people but also the world at large.

In view of all this, then, the judgment at this twenty-fifth anniversary of the establishment of the Republic, taking all things into consideration, must be that great progress has been made in the face of heartbreaking internal obstructions, which have been aggravated by external interference; and that, in addition to material advancement, there has been a remarkable change socially and spiritually which has contributed to the most important of all potential developments—the finding of the voice of China.

2.

SALVATION FROM
WITHIN

"We do not stand in need of any political, social, or economic 'isms,' so long as we can use the experience and wisdom of our forefathers and have the advantage of modern scientific technique."

CHINA lately[8] has been brought forcibly into prominence as a result of spectacular happenings. For example, there have been internal political explosions and the more widespread effects of external aggression and intrigue.

Unfortunately the reading public as a whole has no time to analyze origins of newspaper reports or to focus events in their proper proportions. Distortion consequently triumphs over fact, and the public mind is prone to take it for granted that China produces nothing but startling sensations, mysteries, and make-believe.

The really startling thing about China, however, is the amazing progress that is taking place. The era of civil wars and banditry is now approaching its end. Both the will of the people and the policy of the National Government are

[8] February 21, 1937.

[67]

united in harmonizing, composing, and settling all differences through peaceful means. Public opinion within China is now the strongest factor in deterring the hasty who would rush to settle their differences with the sword.

Everywhere there is widespread recognition of the fact that with the solution of the economic problem the political problem will be automatically solved. For this reason the government is bending its energies toward giving the people an efficient, honest, and progressive administration. Where carelessness and corruption have long held sway this is not so easy as it may at first appear.

The New Life Movement, the third anniversary of which we are celebrating this week, is deeply concerned with the character that goes to make a nation. Without men of character there can be no unified state. When men allow personal ambition, greed, selfishness, and vainglory to dominate their political theories and actions, we are immediately plunged into civil war. There is an old Chinese saying:

"If you are planning for one year, sow grain; if planning for ten years, plant trees, but when planning for a hundred years, grow men."

The work of educators, missionaries, social workers, the various philanthropic foundations, and now of the New Life Movement is deeply concerned with developing men and women of character. As China finds herself being closely knit together into one unified whole she acknowledges a debt of gratitude to her own sons and daughters and to those who have come to us from across the seas.

In addition to building character, the New Life Movement stresses the responsibility and duties of citizenship. Ambitious men may intrigue to invade neighboring provinces but, as citizens are more and more voicing their opinions and insisting upon unification, the breaking of national unity is becoming exceedingly difficult. He is a foolhardy man indeed who today will disregard this growing and formidable public opinion. National unity is here because the people demand it.

Generalissimo Chiang Kai-shek has devoted the greater part of his life to the unification of China's armies and this has been no small undertaking. For some time past he has been turning his attention to the economic and social needs of the people as the next logical step in the modernization of our country.

But before I go on to that fascinating subject, let me devote a few minutes to the remarkable advancement in cultural education that is taking place right before our eyes. This may be the least sensational program of reconstruction, but it is certainly the most far-reaching.

Everywhere in China there seems to be an insatiable thirst for knowledge. Bookstores are crowded; periodicals and magazines are increasing, and newspaper offices are bursting open around us like popcorn. Universities, schools, lecture halls, are all crowded. Popular evening classes for farmers, workers, ricksha pullers, shop assistants, and housekeepers are in full swing in most large centers. All modern findings in hygiene and diet as well as the simpler rules for healthful living are eagerly sought. The radio is being listened to by tens of thousands of our people. We receive fan mail from the remotest corners of our country. Knowledge and unification go hand in hand.

To you in America, Canada, Great Britain, and Europe we are greatly indebted for the part you have played and are still playing in helping us to spread knowledge of the modern world throughout the provinces of China. I wonder if you realize as I do that we are brothers and sisters the world over? Why should there ever be misunderstanding and strife when so many of us hold the same ideals and are working for world peace and progress?

But I must tell you something of what progress we are making toward economic betterment. You know as I do that economic improvement comes more rapidly in times of peace. Generalissimo Chiang Kai-shek has not merely brought the nation peace, and has under the New Life Movement unified all the forces working toward the welfare of the people, but in addition to his military duties he has been working unceasingly on plans for economic betterment. Into the framework of a constitutional system of government will go all these schemes for the development of natural resources and the opening of new avenues of livelihood for the people.

Perhaps the biggest factor in the economic development of the country and the unification of the various provinces is the ever-widening system of highways and railroads that is being pushed into remote parts of the interior. The motorbus is now busy in every province supplementing the donkey, the mule litter, the sedan chair, and the wheelbarrow. Highways now exist so that you may drive an automobile through China from Shanghai to Singapore, as well as through the westernmost province of China to Europe and Great Britain. You can board a train at Canton in the very south of China and ride by rail right through to any point in Europe and Great Britain —the longest railway journey in the world. If you use your imaginations on what this means to China and the other nations of the world, you will have a picture more startling than anything misinformed newspapers and magazines have yet brought to you.

Yesterday, I was examining some samples of soil taken from Lichwan in Kiangsi Province and analyzed by the National Geological Survey Laboratories in Nanking. This forcibly reminded me how greatly scientific methods are being applied in China for economic improvement and how those scientists under the National Government are busily classifying the untapped resources of the country. Such was not possible a few years ago, but China now has her own sons and daughters returning from abroad equipped with the technique and skill for participation in this great task of reconstruction.

Not only are scientists busy at work everywhere, but great engineering projects are under way, especially in connection with flood prevention, river conservancy, and irrigation.

Great efforts are being made to raise the standard of living by systematically developing the natural resources of the country. To do this effectively the Generalissimo launched the People's Economic Reconstruction Movement as complementary to the New Life Movement.

In the midst of all these changes, the New Life Movement supplies us with a spiritual life line to hold on to, while we struggle toward a higher level of living for all our people.

The slogan "Salvation from Within" does not imply a policy of isolation or anything even approaching it. It merely indicates that we have native leadership and technique which did not exist a few years ago. The old system of haphazard philanthropy in China is slowly giving way to better economic planning framed within a thoroughly democratic state. We do not stand in need of any political, social, or economic "isms," so long as we can use the experience and wisdom of our forefathers and have the advantage of modern scientific technique.

We must further see that we appoint to office capable men who are dedicating themselves to living the principles of new life and to working for internal peace and complete co-operation with all the nations who respect us and our inalienable rights of freedom and equality.

3.

UNIFYING CHINA
BY AIR

"He has flown the length and breadth of the country, over rugged mountain, fertile plain, and desert sand, and he has been able to do things of far-reaching importance for the country."

Of all the inventions that have helped to unify China perhaps the airplane is the outstanding one. Its ability to annihilate distance has been in direct proportion to its achievements in assisting to allay suspicion and misunderstanding among provincial officials far removed from one another or from the seat of government.

Prior to the advent of the airplane provincial officials, especially those in far-flung provinces, were almost rulers unto themselves. In the particularly remote provinces they seldom were able to visit the Capital. Exchange of correspondence was almost futile because of the great length of time absorbed in the coming and the going. Nor could the high officials of the Capital ever feel it possible to take

[75]

extended journeys into the interior except at rare intervals. In the old days such journeys not only absorbed considerable time but were full of discomfort, hardships, and inconvenience for the traveling functionary as well as for all the lesser ones through whose territory it was his obligation to pass. Only along the railways and the larger waterways could officials move with anything approximating speed and comfort before the airplane appeared.

How significant has been the influence of air travel on national political and social development, to say nothing of its economic affairs, can be realized by a cursory review of the aerial itineraries of Generalissimo Chiang Kai-shek. He has flown to almost every province of China — journeys that he never could have undertaken in ordinary circumstances. From Nanking to Yunnan and back, via the Yangtze River route, would have taken two months of quick traveltime by the usual means of transportation. Yet now it may be done in one day by airplane. The journey from Chungking to Kweiyang, in Kweichow Province, used to absorb sixteen days of arduous sedan-chair travel and enormous energy. The chair journey from Kweiyang to Yunnan took a similar amount of time, and required as much stamina. Yet the Generalissimo swept over this ocean of mountains by airplane in about one hour and a quarter for the first journey and one hour and a half for the second. Roads are now connecting these points, so travelers who are unable to use airplanes may employ motor-driven vehicles and save themselves, their flesh, their bones, and their nerves the aches and pains produced by weeks in cramping chairs.

It is not necessary to list in detail the almost constant important journeys that have been made by the General-issimo in pursuance of his duties. Suffice it to say that he has flown the length and breadth of the country, over rugged mountain, fertile plain, and desert sand, and he has succeeded in doing things of inestimable value and far-reaching importance for the country by being able, with comparative ease and without loss of time, to meet officials of remote regions in their own yamens, and there solve with them their varied problems, satisfy their minds, and give them assurances of Nanking's close interest in them and their worries.

At the same time he has been able to acquire a work-ing knowledge of the topography and characteristics of the country such as no high official has ever been able to do before; and this, added to his personal contacts with different officials and people, has provided him with un-precedented equipment for the performance of those duties which fall to his lot in the furtherance of his plans in the interests of a better China. And other officials are following his example in more limited but just as impor-tant ways. All of them certainly are demolishing provincial jealousies and establishing relations on a basis of understanding.

What the airplane has done for the Generalissimo in his official work it surely is doing for others in their different fields of activity. China is a country particularly adapted for the utilization of the airplane. Its great distances, the remoteness of enormous regions, the difficulties and slowness of ordinary means of travel combine to make the airplane an increasing necessity for the transportation of mails and passengers to faraway places, as well as to cities that are, in terms of time, comparatively close. With the adjustment of internal affairs in China so that the benefits of unity and peace may be effectively realized will come greater development in the establishment and equipment of airports.

Apart from the airfields that have been constructed at various cities throughout the country, numerous emergency landing fields have been laid down in intermediate regions to make flying safer. Many more will come, and existing fields will be enlarged and improved. As the well-surfaced highway is the *sine qua non* of the modern automobile, so a well-surfaced airfield, equipped with efficient runways, is the *sine qua non* of the fast and up-to-date airplanes now becoming a necessity for both personal and public uses. It was not so long ago that China had neither airplane nor landing ground, but she has augmented her possessions in both as time has gone on, and these it is to be hoped will be but guiding stones of experience along the road of continued progress.

The air-mindedness of the Chinese people is growing greatly, and this augurs well for the future of aviation. Given freedom from disturbances, prosperity will come with leaps and bounds to China. Hand in hand with that desideratum will arrive the need for expanding air services. In time all large cities will have adequate airports and facilities for air traffic, and China will take her rightful place among the best air-served countries in the world.

Section III

NEW SCHOOLS FOR OLD

EDUCATING THE CHILDREN OF
THE REVOLUTION[1]

*"I am convinced that we must train not only
the head, but the heart and hand as well. I
want the students to integrate the virtues of old
China with the vigor and intensity of purpose
needed to reconstruct a better modern China."*

THE fourteenth of November is the anniversary of the
founding in Nanking of the School for Children of the
Chinese Revolution. This school is right in the heart of
Chung-Shan Memorial Park, and in the protective shelter
of Dr. Sun Yat-sen's tomb. Much of my heart is in the
work of this school.

In 1928 the National Government appointed a committee to undertake the education of the children whose
fathers had been killed in the National Revolution. The
families of these fallen heroes had been pensioned, it is

[1] After the commencement of the Sino-Japanese hostilities, the schools
were forced to suspend. The school premises were made base hospitals
for wounded soldiers where the older students remained to serve. Younger students were either returned to their guardians or transferred to
schools in the interior. The cattle, hogs, and poultry, parts of the famous school dairy, were moved to Changsha before the fall of Nanking
and later to Chengtu.

[83]

true. But the government did not feel that their responsibility toward the heroes of the Revolution ended with the establishment of a Memorial Cemetery and Park for those who lost their lives, and the pensioning of those who were left. The government must be father to the children. Nor was it the children of officers who were to be especially favored. Most of the dead were soldiers of the ranks. Their children had less chance of education than the others and so they were given first consideration.

At the first meeting of the committee of interested government officials, Tan Yen-kai, the noted Han-lin scholar (at the time chairman of the government) and a greathearted soul, turned to me and said, "We are ready to give you our moral support, but you will have to take charge of the work!" Perhaps it sounds easy to say, "Go ahead, we will have a school for the children of the revolutionaries!" But things do not come to pass that way. Back of the real success that is ours today stand almost incredible difficulties that had to be overcome and problems that had to be solved.

In the first place, there was no money for such a project. It became my first duty to find sources of government revenue not allocated to a particular purpose and secure approval to pigeonhole these amounts for the school. On this point, suffice it to say that in seven months' time we secured an endowment of a half million dollars. In securing funds I was greatly helped by the efforts of government officials and private individuals whose imagination was fired by this opportunity to do something fundamentally beneficial for the children of the Revolution.

In the second place, the children of the revolutionaries were all over China. They were in Canton and Manchuria, in Hunan and Fukien, in Yunnan and even Sinkiang. When we first sent application blanks to the armies in these various provinces and through them to the families of the fallen, no one came. There was to be no cost to the family for the education of the child, but we did decide that the child would have to remain in the custody of the school from the time of entering until he had finished. Most of them would be far from home, much too far to think of vacations spent at home in the summer. Besides, there was no way of meeting such additional expense. So for several months there was more staff than pupils. But this difficulty, too, passed away. The time came when the school was known far and wide for its high standards and its practical efficiency, and parents other than those of the Revolution — well-to-do people, many of them — wanted to send us their children and pay for their board and tuition. Of course, none of these were accepted. Even so, now we have many thousand more applicants than we can accept.

Another problem loomed large. How was the school to

be so organized that students attending here would not come to feel that they were getting something for nothing? We wanted them to feel their right to be there. Their fathers had died that China might live. The school was theirs. But over and over again when I talked to the students, I said something like this:

"Your fathers died for our country. The government owes you a debt. But it is equally true that the government is in debt to hundreds of thousands of others who are not here. You are the favored few. Therefore, you must do something in turn to repay the government for this opportunity which it has given you. You must justify your being here!"

It was one of my most earnest desires that we should not educate our students in such a way that they would sap the life of the country — a white-collared army that would feel that the world owed them a living.

To this end we organized the school on the industrial plan. We tried to point out the value of learning a trade, of understanding better methods of farming, of helping now in the life of the community, and of going back to the land to share new knowledge with the farmers of one's own neighborhood. Most of our boys come from the farm. We want them to go back to the land with better methods of farming. The high school boys, therefore, work half time in the fields. We have two farms in connection with the school. One is a model farm of 800 mow² with all the most modern machinery. The other is of 200 mow subdivided into small fields to be worked by hand labor. It is obvious why we adopted this plan. We want the boys to know the most modern methods of agriculture. At the same time, we do not want them to think that nothing can be done on the small parcel of land with limited resources and only hand implements. They know now what can be done with fruits and vegetables in small-scale farming. They know the value of better seeds. The boys of the school are raising vegetables and fruits for market in Nanking, and our dairy is the best in the city. Because its reputation for sanitation has already been established, the demand for our milk is greater than our supply at present. Other dairies have to advertise to sell their milk. We have to apologize in the press for our inability to supply the demand. Besides the revenue from our market and dairy produce, we have a nursery garden of thirty or forty mow within the city wall, and the older boys do landscape gardening for people in the city.

Only the children under eight years of age have all the work done for them. Those over eight must wash their clothes, keep their rooms orderly, and help in other school duties. From the fifth and sixth grades on, the boys learn some vocation or a technical trade. They begin by learning

² About 120 acres.

to be call boys, telephone boys, junior secretaries, advancing from one phase of training to another and more difficult one. For the older ones there are trades. We have carpentry and towel making. We are contemplating basket weaving and a small cannery to take care of our surplus fruits and vegetables. We hope to offer a number of trades, requiring each student to go through all, and learn three fully, so that he can choose the one best suited to his ability and interest. We anticipate a time when the industries and projects of the school will make it entirely self-supporting. When that time comes, the funds now used for this school can be used for others organized on similar lines. This one is still experimental, but, profiting by our experience, there must be many more such someday for China.

I have my own theories of education. I have had opportunity to put them to the test. I have corrected some and learned others. But I am still convinced that we must train not only the head, but the heart and hand as well. Our students need a better understanding of life and higher standards of living, but not beyond the practical. They must not be educated to be discontented with the life to which they will return. They must not come to feel that school alone is life. I want them to help build the right kind of social structure. I want them to be able to integrate the virtues of old China with the vigor and intensity of purpose needed to reconstruct a better modern China.

We make earnest efforts, too, to train the teachers, so that they may enter into the real spirit of the school. We follow the cottage system, two or more teachers occupying a cottage with thirty or forty boys. It means practically twenty-four hours a day on duty. But we are continually impressing on our teachers that they are "in loco parentis." To make good they must enter into the spirit of the place.

On one point I am adamant. Perhaps I am considered undiplomatic. But I do not believe in mixing politics with education. At one time many applicants expected to be appointed because of influential recommendation. I decided that, regardless of who recommended, teachers would be accepted only on their qualifications. Either the Dean or I have a personal interview with every teacher considered, and every teacher is put on probation for one semester. He or she must make good, for reputations and recommendations cannot run a school. Sometimes I have felt compelled to say, "The school is to be run solely for the good of the students. It is not to be made a convenient dumping place for teaching failures. Either I run the school and take the responsibility, or else relieve me of responsibility and run it some other way!" Of late I have received no more letters of recommendation. To the teachers I often say, "It is comparatively easy to be heroic on the battlefield. There one can make a glorious gesture with one's life. But the real test of moral character is willingness to keep on day after day, week in and week out, year passing year, with humdrum routine because it is one's work and one's duty!"

I have referred to training head and heart and hand — a threefold program. How do we reach the heart and make a permanent contribution to richer living? One way is through our Rural Social Service Club. I have had great joy in organizing the older boys into this group. Whenever I am in Nanking they meet with me once a week. But the work goes on in my absence too. The students go to the farmers, make friends with them, give them better seeds, hold for them a monthly entertainment of movies or original plays. It is not unusual to have a thousand country people attending these entertainments. This spring the boys made a rural survey of the fifteen neighboring villages, and through it got an intimate knowledge of the home life of these farmers. It is a superstition in that district not to let outsiders know the names of their children. But each of these boys came to know ten or more families well enough to call the children by other names than that of "Little Pussy" or "Little Puppy." If they had no real name, the boys gave them one.

The boys have organized a school for the children of

the farmers. From four to five-thirty each afternoon they teach them reading and arithmetic, Chinese, and health habits. A doctor comes out twice a week to hold a clinic. The boys have made free medicine available. At first I contributed the money for the medicine. Then I put it up to the boys to think out their own method of paying for it. They thought and thought. I made no suggestions. It was an odd source of revenue which they hit upon, but it paid the bills. They saw the surrounding country overgrown with rushes and reeds. These they cut themselves, and sold in little bunches for firewood. Their clinic goes on with free medicine for the country people. And the boys themselves are making this service possible.

Great emphasis is put on personal neatness and cleanliness of the school and its surroundings. Suggestions are often made in the fifteen-minute assembly period, and inspection of the school takes place twice daily. It has been hard to make both pupils and teachers realize the importance of a high standard in this regard. But I feel that it is little things that tell the story. When wastepaper is allowed to lie about the grounds, when broken panes of glass are not repaired, it usually indicates slackness in larger things as well. A broken pane of glass or a hole in the fence is nothing in itself, but it is ofttimes indicative of the character of the school.

I have written much more in detail about the boys'

work because much of the above applies to the work with the girls as well. The school started as a coeducational institution. We soon felt that the girls needed a somewhat different training. They are now housed in an old yamen inside the city wall. A hundred mow of land, however, has been allotted for their new building which will soon be erected. The plans are now being drawn.

We have four hundred boys in the one school, with room for one hundred more. There are one hundred and fifty girls in the other, with accommodations for about fifty more to come. The numbers could easily be filled, but we allow six months to elapse after an application is made before we give that place to another. Sometimes the child proves too young. Sometimes the difficulties of travel alone are too great.

Up to the fifth grade the girls also have only to attend to their studies. From the fifth and sixth grades on, some home training is given. And in the junior high school they begin on plain sewing, simple cooking, then stocking making, embroidery, making their own clothes and making toys for sale. The girls in the school make all the stockings that are worn, and now have such a surplus that recently I purchased five hundred pairs from them to give to an orphanage in Shanghai.

The brilliant students, both boys and girls, are given opportunity elsewhere. Several of the boys have been sent to college. One who showed marked ability has been sent to an art school and is doing very well. Several of the girls have been sent on to middle school for further academic training, and one is in training as a nurse in Central Hospital, Nanking. The staff there say, "If you have more like her, you may send them without expense." She is already president of the Student Government Association in the training school and is making a fine record in every way.

There are more problems connected with running a school that I have not gone into here. I have said nothing about the difficulty of feeding and clothing these students who do not go home even for the replenishment of their wardrobes. We have had to experiment with cloth to find out what kind wears best. We have learned that it is economy in the end to pay a few more cents per yard than to get the cheapest grade. We have experimented with food and decided that it pays to give good food. The food costs $6 per month per child. The total expenses for one month for food, education, clothing, and overhead come to about $24 per student. When I visit the school I try the food myself. If a work is to succeed, I find that one must look after the details personally and not relegate them to another. One teacher is required to sit at each table, for table manners are an essential part of the training.

Because we give good food and buy good material for clothing, there may be criticism to the effect that we are accustoming the children to standards above the "common people" amongst whom most of them will live. But balanced diets cut down the sick list, and give increased physical endurance and mental vigor. A more firmly knit grade of cloth stands more washings, and a pair of leather shoes outwears several pairs of cloth shoes costing the same amount. These are things worth learning. With such practical knowledge, the students will lift the standard of living in the communities where they later live.

When I am absent the administration rests with the Supervisor who meets every week with the Joint Committee, including the Deans from the faculties of the two schools. Mr. Fu Huei-kuan, General Secretary of the Memorial Park, an agricultural expert and a member of the Board of Trustees, meets with them and his help has been invaluable. Everything done in my absence is submitted for my correction or approval when I return. Or, if I am away for some little time, regular reports are sent that I may revise or approve.

It must be quite obvious that what I said at the beginning is a real conviction with me. To my mind, it is not enough to launch a project and tell somebody to go and see it through. What you would have well done, you must do yourself. You cannot leave it to others. Occasional brilliant strokes do not accomplish as much as the steady wielding of the brush. I have seen so many with education and years of training fail, that I feel education *per se* is useless. I think often of the first principal of McTyeire Girls' School in Shanghai. She was a woman of high school education only, but she made McTyeire. Why? Because she had vision, moral courage and convictions, judgment, and intensity of purpose. These traits spell success. As soon as one works for personal glory the work suffers. Only work for the sake of the work itself and the good it can do deserves success.

In this work I myself have learned a lot. Theories must be tried out and adjusted to the actual needs. They are not absolutes. Into this school for the children of the revolutionary heroes I have put my heart. I feel richly rewarded, and the end is not yet. Purple Mountain and the Sun Yat-sen Memorial are in daily sight of the students. Who knows what inspiration they may imbibe? Who knows if out of the hundreds of boys who will enter and leave our school there may not be at least one Sun Yat-sen? Even one would make it all worth while.

Section IV

LEAVES FROM A BOOK OF TRAVELS

I.

WONDERS OF CHINA'S
SOUTHWEST

*Pen pictures of the rugged loveliness of
the remote southwestern provinces and of
their rich human and industrial resources.*

I

I AM now a long way from you, but I think of you
always.[1] As I travel far and wide about this great country
of ours and see the conditions under which so many of our
people live I think how fortunate you are that you are living comfortably and are being educated so that you can
make your way in the world to your own betterment, and
can help others. Indeed, you are very lucky to have the
splendid chance that you are having, and I am very happy
that you are able to have it.

Now I will tell you something of this great country of
ours. You know that Kweiyang is the capital of Kweichow

[1] While accompanying the Generalissimo when he was leading the bandit suppression campaign in the southwest provinces in 1935, Madame
Chiang found time to write to the students in the school for the children
of revolutionary heroes in Nanking.

[99]

Province, a province that is mostly mountains and is poor and very difficult to reach. Or it used to be difficult. Now there is a motor road from Kwangsi, and soon there will be one from Changsha and another from Chungking, in Szechwan. Soon, too, there will be an air-mail service. Only a short while ago all travel was over stone paths climbing the mountains and descending the valleys. It took seventeen days to get from here to Chungking, and about the same time to get to Canton or Yunnan, and one had to travel by chair or walk. There are mountains everywhere. Not great ranges, but a higgledy-piggledy mass of cone-like hills, some very curious to look at. When we were flying from Chungking here we saw these cones lying in long rows as if some giant had put them there to play with, as children make little hills of sand. When that came about I do not know, but possibly in the time of volcanic action when the crust of the earth was being formed and getting cold. Kweiyang City is in a valley surrounded by these curious hills. It is over 3,000 feet higher than Nanking, so is very cold at this time, whereas you probably feel the summer coming on. Here the trees are just getting their new leaves, the birds are building their nests, and make a great clatter with their chatter and their song. There are different trees and birds here from what you might see in Nanking, and the people also are different.

Mostly the people wear turbans, and there are also

many tribespeople here, the Miaos, who live in the mountains and do hard work on very simple food. They dress differently from the other people; they are shorter and sturdier. They do not smoke opium, and they work hard. Their food is chiefly corn.

Around about us are bandit bands. It is to try and suppress them that the Generalissimo came here. At present they are but twenty miles away from us, but they will be defeated in the end, and then we will really be able to do something to help all the people and make our country strong and great. And that is what you students always must remember — that you are being educated solely to be of help to your country and your fellow men.

Now I will tell you something of our travels. To get here we used steamers, motorcars and airplanes. From Kiukiang I went by steamer to Chungking, which is in Szechwan, and is some 1,350 miles from Shanghai, and some 600 feet higher than Nanking. Really the steamer climbs up that height through the rapids of the Upper Yangtze. Up to Ichang the river is just a great body of water running strongly and eating its way into the fields on either side and carrying lots of good earth out to sea, making the ocean yellow for some sixty miles out, so strong is the current of the river, so great is the quantity of silt (that is, earth) that it carries.

Just after leaving Ichang we come into the famous

Gorges. The river has, through the centuries, eaten its way through the mountains, and sometimes the cliffs are over 1,000 feet high, some of the mountain-tops being as high as 4,000 feet. How strong the river is, what power it possesses can be seen as the steamer drives up against it, and one sees what mighty work the rushing water has done on the rocks. Sometimes they are just straight walls on either side, with the river rushing deep and menacing between, making whirlpools and eddies and currents that are sometimes almost too strong for the steamer engines to work against. Some of the rapids roar in tumult and are very dangerous. These the steamer climbs, throbbing and panting, and — almost stopping. It is all very exciting, for one wonders if the steamer will manage to make the ascent, and it is a climb, one rapid having to be negotiated upwards some six or seven feet in fifty yards. Steamers often get wrecked because the savage river literally takes them and throws them against the jagged and cruel rocks, and woe betide any people who get thrown into the river. They are swept down in the great roaring whirlpools and are lost.

Before the steamers were made to fight their way through this powerful water the junks had to be hauled by men, taking weeks to get through the Gorges alone. Twenty and thirty men hauling on great ropes made of plaited bamboo strips dragged the junks slowly and patiently, most times working like animals, with bare feet clinging to the rocks, and often wearing no clothes. Now that steamers have come such big junks are not used to go against the stream, but all the small ones have to be hauled, or tracked, as they call it, against the strong current, the trackers having to struggle along a narrow path cut in the rocks of the Gorges. If they fall they are lucky if they are not drowned.

The Gorges are very beautiful in the sunlight, and while in them one can fully appreciate the greatness and the grandeur of nature. Upstream from Wanhsien, which is west of the Gorges, the character of the country changes and we pass day after day through rolling hills, all cultivated, the farmhouses being different from those we are used to, and much like the style, as to the roof, that is seen in middle Europe. It is very picturesque landscape, and rich looking.

This upper part of the river is known as the River of Golden Sand, because gold is found in the sand, which is black because of its volcanic origin. As we passed bank after bank of boulders and sand we saw gangs of men heaving away the stones and washing the sand to get the gold out of it. There are five men in each gang. One carries water from the river in two wooden buckets; three throw the boulders clear and dig up the sand in which the gold dust is found (called paydirt), and one works a basket into which the earth is tipped and over which the water is thrown. The water washes the dirt on to a large board about three feet six inches long and three feet broad, the surface of which is made into fine ripples, as they are called in the gold-washing industry, but much like a foreign-style washboard. The sand is washed over this board and the gold, being heavier than the sand, is caught by the ripples.

One night we anchored near a bank where gold seekers were working. Some of the passengers went ashore and saw a "cleanup," as it is called, of one gang. After working all the afternoon they washed out of the ripples about one pound of black sand. They then put that sand not in a tin dish but in a wooden tray which they gently moved about till the sand was washed out and left behind a fine line of "color," or gold dust. There was not much, however, and the workers sold it to one passenger for one silver dollar. So for one afternoon's work they got just twenty cents each. Not a rich showing, by any means. If they have luck, they might find more gold dust, and even a nugget. Sometimes they do get a chance and find a nugget which is valuable according to its size. There is a great possibility of making this industry worth something to the country if modern methods of getting out the gold are employed. It is hoped that will soon be done so that the country can find a lot of work for the people and in time get strong again as it used to be in olden days. Hundreds of miles farther up the Yangtze there are great areas of alluvial soil which will, someday, be worked by dredgers.

When we got to Chungking it was raining, the first rain since leaving Nanchang. We had to climb high flights of wide stone steps to get to the roadway. We went to live in a big house which the Generalissimo and I did not like because it was not built from honest money. It belongs to a militarist, like many others here. It is sad to say that Szechwan, which is one of the richest provinces in our country, is made poor by the greed of men who get into power and rob the people for their own profit. These militarists are ignorant, and do not know what patriotism means. That is what you students must learn and understand. If you do not, then China will never recover. You must always try to teach others what the country is, what the flag stands for, and what all good citizens should do — that is, work honestly to help the country become strong and great.

In Szechwan, and in Kweichow, as in several other provinces in the west, the people are made poor by opium. The bad officials have poppies grown and make great profits from shipping opium out. This evil will kill China if it is not stopped. Therefore, the Generalissimo and I, wherever we go, speak strongly against the evil and we work to educate the people to do their best to have the opium stopped so that our race shall not become slaves.

In Chungking we persuaded the high officials to shut up the opium shops, and I am trying to organize the women to work against the evil. The difficulty is that they do not know how to organize anything, or have meetings, and this is one thing I want the girl students to remember. They must try their best to prepare themselves to grow up competent to form societies to do good, to hold meetings, and get things done. At present the illiterate women think that they have to talk about this and that and everything except the one thing they ought to talk about and do. That is not their fault so much as it is their misfortune. They had no chance to be educated, as you girls have, and therefore they are more to be pitied than blamed. But you can learn a valuable lesson from them, for as time goes on, our women are going to do their share in saving their country. You must, therefore, try to understand things so that you can teach others what to do and how to do it when you get the chance.

In Szechwan there is a great opportunity for the people to recover themselves, for their province is rich in vegetation, as well as in other products. But there has been no systematic development there, as in some other provinces. Lack of development of natural resources is one reason why China is poor and weak. If you look at the great countries of the world you will see that they are strong because they have developed their mining and

other industries to make the things they want, and to
give employment to their people. In China most of the
work is done on farms, and we have to spend our money
buying other things that we need from foreign countries.
This is not right. Consequently, the Generalissimo and
I are working hard to have a new movement started to
develop the natural resources of the country, start industries to manufacture the necessities we must have, and
improve agriculture so that we can grow all we need to
eat. This movement will be the People's Economic Reconstruction Movement, and we want all of you students
to understand what it means to China. It means that if
China takes lessons from the good foreign countries she
in time can be strong and powerful, and can get rich too.
Also no one will dare to take advantage of her and rob
her of her territory. But we must all work hard and educate
the people to understand the reasons for such a new movement. All of us want our country to be strong and rich,
and that is the means by which it can be done. There is
no magic about it. Riches are not conjured out of a magician's hat. They have to be worked for. We must be wise
and open up our country. If we do not we will surely
become the slaves of some other country who wants to
take what we have. The Generalissimo is doing his utmost
out here to teach the officials and the people what they
must do. In that work of teaching everyone must help.

By and by, I will tell you more about the interesting things in Szechwan. So far we have been only to Chungking. It is a city built on a high hill at the junction of two rivers — the Yangtze Kiang and the Kialing. Long flights of steps lead up from the water; up and down go the travelers, jostling with the carriers of water and the bearers of freight. Now there is a motor road, and many wide streets at the top. Five years ago there were no wheeled vehicles here. Now there are many motorcars and hundreds of rickshas. Previously people rode in chairs, carried by coolies. The main road goes to Chengtu, the capital, and people can travel there in two days. Just a little while ago it took weeks to do the journey. This is a long letter so I must close with good wishes and hopes that you will work hard so that you all can help our country.

II

When last I wrote to you I was in Kweiyang, but now I am far away from that spot. I am in Chengtu, an old capital, made famous at the time of the Three Kingdoms.

I told you about Kweiyang. It is set in a small valley surrounded by numerous conelike hills, on the top of some of which are temples surrounded by cool groves of trees. At the south of the city a clear water stream flows, and twists and turns away into the hills. We found another clear stream some miles from the city where the Generalissimo and I used sometimes to walk. It winds itself through a pretty little gorge known as the Dragon Gate. Someone carved the characters high on a cliff. The legend has it that all the water of the stream ran into a cave and disappeared, but that was not quite true. We saw the cave and we saw some water running into it, but the rest of the stream crawled like a dragon through the narrow valley between the hills. Beautiful wild roses — like dark-red velvet — festooned the rocks in places, and ferns and flowers grew elsewhere, making the spot as pretty as it was quiet, for no one lived there.

Farther out from Kweiyang, about twenty miles, in a region the bandits went through, we found another delightful stream alongside of which azaleas grew in abundance and of a beautiful red color. The hills hereabouts are, as elsewhere in the province, conical-shaped, a formation which generally rendered it difficult for our troops to surround the bandits.

In due course the time came for us to leave. We went to the airfield and boarded an airplane which took us high over the mountains to Yunnanfu, now called Kunming. About sixty miles from Kweiyang we saw the river tumbling in a beautiful waterfall over a cliff about two hundred feet high. It raced into a deep ravine. Someday, maybe, the water will be used as power for the development of electricity. The mountains are high here and the gorges are deep. Low down in one we saw an old suspension bridge made of chains, over which the old trail passes to and from Yunnanfu and Kweiyang.

When we got to Kutsingfu we were over the high ranges, and Yunnan was below us. Here the soil is very red, and there is much cultivation. We saw motor roads built and being built. Soon they will connect with Kweiyang, whence a road already runs west almost to the Yunnan border. In the deep ravines it is difficult to build a road; but it will be done in time. By October, it is hoped that a traveler will be able to get into his car at Shanghai and drive all the way to Kweiyang and Kunming, and also from Kweiyang to Chengtu, as well as to Kwangsi and other places.

Flying over the red soil of Yunnan we came to the plain on which Kunming stands. There we saw rows of dark-green trees crawling over the country like big long dragons. They mark the old canals, dug centuries ago by wise people, which are still supplying water for the fields. When we reached Kunming we could see the Provincial Chairman's house on a hill, while on another stood Yunnan University, a spacious pink-colored building. In the latter we stayed while in the city.

We landed at the airfield, on which was a colorful marquee. A large crowd of people was there to welcome us — high officials, the foreign consular body, and Chinese civilians. All along the road to the city were crowds of students, mostly dressed in white, though some were in blue. When we passed through the city gates and began traversing the streets we saw thousands of people crowding the footpaths and lots of flags hung out together with big red lanterns. Kunming streets are clean and well kept. In the main street the houses are all of one type in one section, and of another type in an adjoining section. They look very effective, better than the higgledy-piggledy assortments of badly designed houses that we see in some other places. And it is to be noted, the people are taught to walk on one side of the street going one way, and on the other side going the other way.

The people of Yunnan Province, like the people of Kweichow, are very picturesque. The country people wear the colorful clothes of former times. The women wear red trousers, embroidered jackets, and big picturesque hats. There are also tribespeople, the Lolos, sometimes in the streets and now and again some Miaos. The latter are distinctive especially the "Flowery Miao," who get their name from the attractive, flower-embroidered clothes they wear. They all favor prodigious pleated skirts. These I saw in Kweichow.

Generally speaking, the climatic conditions were better than Kweiyang, which was damp and cold. One night the school children, numbering many thousands, gave a lantern procession. It was strikingly effective. There were many beautiful lanterns and many curious ones. Plenty of representations of airplanes appeared, in all colors and designs; there were crabs and fishes and strange animals; there were lots and lots of flowers and baskets, as well as buckets, birds, vegetables, and other things. It took a long time for the procession to pass, and, as the children had to climb long flights of steps to get to the entrance doors near where we were seated they were puffing and blowing. But they got a lot of fun out of it. The procession of vari-colored lanterns could be seen a long way off — winding and twining through the night, sinuously like a serpent.

Near Kunming is a mountain, known as Hsi Shan, where there are some old, picturesque, and big temples. At the foot of the mountain is a large, deep lake, said to be the largest fresh-water lake in China. We went by motorcar close to the mountain; then went by chairs the rest of the way, up hill and down dale, and through the bamboo groves.

At one temple we saw a large crypt where were stored jars and vases containing the ashes of the priests who had died. The bodies were cremated, and this crypt held hundreds of urns of ashes. Perhaps cremation is better than burial, especially in China where so much valuable land is wasted by graves. In Central China, and in other parts, too, the people bury their dead on their farm lands. This is not good, for it takes up land that could grow crops. In Szechwan and Kweichow they are wiser, for they bury their dead on hillsides that cannot be cultivated. Near some cities the burial places are great cemeteries. Each grave, or nearly every one, has a headstone. This system of burial ensures a great saving of good arable land, and it is a wise practice. The priests perhaps do a still wiser thing by cremating their dead, and keeping their ashes in the porcelain vases in the crypt.

There is one temple,—or many temples, in fact, clustered together,—on the steep side of the mountain near a high cliff overlooking the lake. At the top a tunnel has been driven through the solid rock to get to a cave, which has been ornamented by carvings of Buddhas. The tunnel leads out into the open at one spot. A balustrade has been cut to prevent one falling down a thousand feet. The lake extends a long way, and beyond are mountains painted purple by the evening sunlight.

It was a long descent down stone stairways to the lake-side. A little steamer was waiting for us. We reached it in sampans rowed by girls in their picturesque red trousers and light-blue jackets. The steamer took us across the lake back to Kunming. We landed at a park, well laid out, with nice buildings which were well kept.

A narrow canal runs from the lake some distance

toward the city. It is a channel of navigation for junks and sampans. I saw many carrying stone and other cargo from the remote side of the lake. All the boats were rowed by women or girls. I saw several, however, being pushed through the thick mud by little boys. They thought it great fun, but it was hard and dirty work. I felt sorry that they did not have a chance to be in a clean school instead of having to work while so young, in such a dirty place as a narrow muddy canal.

Yet they are not so badly off as the thousands of little children who have to work in the tin mines at Kochin. These little ones, mostly between 8 and 14, are, I am told, sent thousands of feet under the ground, through narrow tunnels only big enough for their little bodies to crawl. They dig out the tin, and then have to carry it out. The temperature is so hot underground that they often faint when they get to the cool air, and many of them die of pneumonia and other diseases. There is so little water there that they can seldom have a wash, to say nothing of a regular bath, so they take ox bones and scrape the dirt off their little bodies. The bones are also supposed to be a charm to ward off evil. The children have a hard and difficult life, and get little pay for it.

The Generalissimo is trying to have child labor stopped, and just think how lucky you boys and girls are to be in a well-kept, clean school, having good food, and time for play when you are free from lessons in the classroom. When you think you have big grievances you should always remember the poor children of our country who have no chance to go to school, or get an education, or have good food, but who have to work hard in bad and unhealthy surroundings. Never forget these poor, unfortunate children when you fancy you have something to complain about. Then, I feel sure, you will not complain.

If you remember your geography you will know that south of Yunnan is Indo-China. It is all hot, tropical country. From Indo-China to Kunming there is a railway. It is narrow-gauge (not so wide as the railways in China) and the line follows the valleys because the mountains are high and rugged. I wanted to go and look at the tropics, so started off one day from Kunming at a little after the noon hour. I did not go by a train, but by what looked like a motorbus running on the rails. It was driven by gasoline and ran on rubber tires. It went fast over the rails—twisting and turning—and, for me, the journey was not only uncomfortable, but made me very brain-sick. The temperature got hotter and hotter.

Kunming itself, as I mentioned before, is some 6,000 feet above sea level, and not far away from the city the line climbed over a ridge which is the highest point on the railway, over 7,000 feet. As we glided down the other side we saw three beautiful blue, or green, lakes, set in red country. They were the only things which looked cool and inviting.

We traveled downgrade through numerous tunnels, round curves along precipices, and through picturesque gorges, the torrent roaring and rushing below us or by us all the time. The farther we went down the valleys the hotter it became and the more tropical the vegetation grew. Bamboos and bananas appeared, and in one narrow gorge we were told that monkeys abounded. On the return journey one of the party actually saw a monkey on a bush. The monkey he saw was so excited to see the car that he shook the bush like a mad thing. I suppose the little fellow wondered what the rushing monster was.

We stayed at Amichow for the night, at a sort of hotel. The temperature was so warm and the air so damp that I decided not to go any farther down the railway, for the farther south we went the lower dropped the altitude and the higher mounted the heat. Also I was told that the line wiggled worse than before and would be too uncomfortable, especially since I had not been feeling well for some time. Next morning we started back, and were in Kunming after one o'clock. We would have been earlier, but a tire blew out and we had to wait until a new one was put on. The air was so cool at Kunming that it was like balm after the heat of the valleys through which we had just ascended.

The Generalissimo flew to Kweiyang, and on to Chungking. I left by airplane for Chungking direct two days later. We flew due north from Kunming to the Yangtze River, over a countryside of bright red, orange, purple, brown, and other colors, which, with varied greens of the vegetation, looked like a gorgeous painting. But there were heavy clouds, and we had to dodge up the valleys till we reached the Yangtze. We came to the river near Kiaosi, where the Yangtze touches the southernmost point in the whole of its course. You can see it on a map, where it takes a dip down into Yunnan. Then we flew high over the clouds (14,000 ft.) to get smooth air, till we were past the Taliangshan ranges, one that we flew by being 16,000 ft. above the sea.

Far away to our left was Ningyuanfu, recently besieged by the bandits on their way into northern Szechwan, and still farther to the westward was the great high country of the Lolo tribesmen. Some who have traveled in this rarely visited region tell me that there are great rolling spaces reminiscent of the Canadian wheatlands. The Lolo tribespeople do not welcome strangers, however, nor did they, for a very long time, want to have anything to do with our officials. They used to be treated badly, but in these enlightened days life will be better for them. They like their independence. They are described as tall, muscular people, the women being attractive and cleanly dressed, and the men being distinctive by reason of what looks like a horn protruding from the top of their foreheads. In reality it is their hair twisted with a turban to look like a horn, from six to nine inches long, and is supposed by them to resemble that of the fabled unicorn. The women affect little jackets and long, flounced, and pleated petticoats, which trail to their heels and which they like to swirl vigorously as they walk about. They plait their hair in two long tails which they wind about their heads. It is interesting to know that travelers observe that the women hold a highly respected place in the tribe. The country which these aloof people inhabit is all mountainous and remote, and approximates some 10,000 square miles. Perpetual snow peaks grace their landscape, and beyond them is the great rampart of Tibet.

As we flew past the high peaks near Ningyuan the clouds developed into a bank that looked solid enough to stand upon, and the pilot decided to fly back and get underneath them. So back we went for fifty miles till we found a hole in the clouds through which we could corkscrew down till we were in the valley of the Yangtze, between great high mountains. We followed the river under the clouds till we reached Chungking. Through the narrow valley made by these mountains the plane flew fast. We seemed to be in danger of our wing-tips striking rocks or farmhouses. Sometimes we passed through rainstorms which blotted out sight of everything, but we got through safely. The mountains average in height about ten thousand feet; their sides are cultivated and dotted with houses, perched high on the sides of the ravine. If the people fell out their front doors they would risk tumbling thousands of feet into the river below. Wherever possible the mountainsides are terraced for cultivation, some of the terraces running to eight and more thousand feet—just like wide runged ladders.

Far down below the river tore through its narrow confines, a sheer torrent, and no junks were seen navigating it till we got near Suifu, now called Ipin. Ipin is at the end of the old caravan trail from Kunming to Chengtu, and is situated at the junction of the Yangtze and the Min River, which flows southward from Chengtu. Ipin is a clean-looking city, with good streets. Here the high mountains end. We met many bad rainstorms in this vicinity, in one of which we could not see anything at all. We had to swing round and round in as small a circle as possible so as to keep from hitting any hill that might be about.

When we got out of the storm we found ourselves cruising over a river which proved to be the Lu Ho. It enters the Yangtze near Luchow. Soon we were at Luchow, which has a high clock tower and a big square-based stupa decorating its center. It was soon out of sight, for we were now going downriver fast, and we arrived at

Chungking before eleven o'clock. We had left Kunming about eight o'clock.

I forgot to tell you that just before we reached Ipin we saw a beautiful blue lake high among the pine-covered mountain peaks. The lake was still and looked deep, and apparently no one lives near it. I saw no signs of life. The peaks surrounding it are steep and afford no foothold for farms. A little farther on we saw that all the houses were towers. They looked like blockhouses three stories high. Many were partly destroyed, as if they had suffered from fighting. I suppose in this difficult and distant region there has been a lot of trouble in the past, compelling the people to devise permanent defenses, so they decided to live in towers to protect themselves. The country is mountainous and wild and high above the rushing river. I found out later that the inhabitants of the region are tribespeople. The towers that I saw were in the south of Szechwan, in difficult mountain country along the Yangtze, but similar ones, perhaps a little more pretentious, exist over wide areas in the northwest of Szechwan. An "Englishman's home is said to be his castle," but each family of these tribesmen of remote China has a real castle of its own—a castle like those in the fairy stories. They are from two to four stories high with embrasures, loopholes, and no window or opening (so far as I could observe when studying those I flew by) less than ten or twelve feet from the ground. I could see no way of getting into them except by the use of a ladder, but I may be mistaken, since study from an airplane has its disadvantages. One writer says the castles in the north of the province sprang from an old feudal system which existed among the tribesmen, and which the Chinese destroyed in time to the benefit of all concerned. Well, we must hope so.

We stayed in Chungking for the day and left for Chengtu next afternoon. We flew over the famous Red Basin, which is said to be the heaviest populated region in the world. It looks as if the country had the measles — red blotches of hills surrounded by khaki-colored water, which are paddy fields. As far as the eye could reach it was this kind of landscape, all the red hills being cultivated, and not a piece of land visible that was not growing something or holding a farmhouse, a village, a town, or a city. Then we went under what looked like a dangerous storm — a line squall — the clouds being black and low and threatening. But we got through all right and came to a ridge of mountains over which we flew and found stretched before us the plain of Chengtu, quite different from the Red Basin, in color, though also heavy with cultivation. Canals were everywhere, radiating from the famous ancient irrigation system beginning to the west at Kwanhsien. This irrigation system was founded by a Chinese official named Li-ping, and his son, some two thousand years ago, and is famous throughout the world, for it was so well planned and built that for all these centuries it has been giving life to this great plain and Red Basin. These wise men had a channel cut through the Li-tu hill to lead the waters of the Min River by several main canals, spread fanwise from the source, to the vast region of which Chengtu is the center. At the present day those canals look like original rivers and are mapped as such, but the lateral canals, which spread all over the country and irrigate it still work with their locks as in the days of old. No wonder that this part of our country grows four crops of lush vegetation a year. Let us hope that those responsible for dissipating the benefits which can be derived from this old system will mend their ways and that prosperity will soon return to this rich, though distant, province.

We found Chengtu sprawled on the plain, not square like some cities, but with walls following the contours of the country. It is a large city for one so far in the interior, and has had a past packed full of historic interest. It seemed to our flying eyes to be packed full of houses and the streets were full of people looking up at us as the airplane glided round and round the city. Then we landed and drove into the city to the place prepared for us. The streets we saw were full of shops, and we could see many handicrafts being followed, workers in brass and bone and bamboo. They were making all manner of things, and were all very busy.

III

The Red Basin was so called by a German geologist, Baron Richthofen, because of the red rock with which it abounds. It is about 100,000 square miles in area. Great mountains surround it on all sides, while the Yangtze River rushes through it from west to east at its southern end. In fact, the Yangtze made the basin. It is said by scientists to have been a lake in remote ages, the waters of which were drained off by the Yangtze cutting a channel some thousands of feet deep through the mountains. Where billions of fishes no doubt thrived in ancient times farmers now live by the million. After the waters went off with their fishes the aborigines came. They, too, died out or departed ages ago. Only signs in caves show that they existed at all.

One foreign writer on this part of our country says that "the whole of the Red Basin is a lasting monument to Chinese genius and industry in matters agricultural." Here are grown rice, maize, millet, sweet potatoes, sugar cane, tobacco, wheat, rape, peas, broad beans, cabbages, and fruits of different kinds, the oranges being famous for their juice and their cheapness. Silk is made everywhere, and is worn by most people here, but cotton is difficult to grow.

While we Chinese are spoken of so highly as agriculturists, we must realize that we do not know everything. We have a lot to learn. Science has been taken advantage of in Western countries to improve crops and plants. We must do that in China. Old ways are well enough, but we could grow more and better crops and fruit by taking intelligent advantage of experiences in foreign countries. We should always look and learn, for we have wonderful foundations for prosperity and wealth if we would only improve upon them. What has suited our ancestors need not be accepted as suitable for us. Times have changed; so have manners. Living is a much more l.. -ic business in these modern times. If we want to use motorcars and trucks and modern inventions we must improve our standard of living to be able to pay for them. Sticking to a wooden shovel, as an example, because our forefathers might have used one, will not get us along very far. The same thing holds for everything. We must improve not only agriculture, but also methods of mining. In fact, we should seek to better everything we do for our livelihood. For progressive people nothing is ever good enough. They always try to improve things. We must do that. You young people should always bear that in mind and make it a rule to try to do something better than anyone else.

In the Red Basin are the great salt deposits, especially at Tze-liu-ching and Wu-ting-chiao. At the former place the people bore holes as deep as 3,000 feet to get the brine up. They do the boring in the old primitive way — an example of what I have just been writing to you — and it is a long and tedious job. They use a heavy iron bar for a drill, attach it to a plaited bamboo rope, drop the drill into the earth till it cuts away a little earth, haul it up again by means of a large wheel, or drum, turned by a bullock, then drop it again, and keep on drop, drop, dropping for years to make a hole two or three thousand feet deep. But after centuries of this the little spark of progress is being seen there, for I am told an attempt is being made to use mechanical power of some sort.

At Tze-liu-ching, in particular, natural gas often comes from the earth instead of brine, but it is useful to heat the iron vats in which the brine is put for evaporation. When the water is boiled off salt is left deposited in the vat in the form of a dirty cake. I have seen donkeys and porters carrying such cakes in various provinces. I saw them in distant Kweiyang and in Kunming, having been carried over terrible mountain paths for hundreds of miles. I wished to go to Tze-liu-ching but was too ill to take the journey. One can travel much of the distance by motorcar, but a chair has to be used some of the way. Only a few years ago there were no other means of overland transport in this province than ponies and chairs. The chairs for long-distance travel are simple structures made of bamboo—two poles, to which is hung a kind of hammock made of slats of bamboo. They are to be seen everywhere, most of the travelers stretching out in them, their bedding on the slats, and above the passenger a long strip of cotton cloth to keep off the direct heat of the sun.

Chengtu, while it has an interesting history, has not much to see when compared with big cities in other parts of China. It has a high wide wall, which is about nine miles around. I think I have, at different times, walked most of it. This wall was the only place where the Generalissimo and I could walk. The city streets are too crowded and too narrow for comfort. The only open space is on the wall, which is about thirty-five feet high and forty feet wide at the top.

Round each side of the city runs a swift stream. All the streams here run full and fast. Canals are everywhere. They are all part of the irrigation system. Strong-looking bridges and bunding made of great stone slabs are noticeable. The people here follow an old rule. It is "dig the bed deep, keep the banks low." And they do. Every year silt is removed from all the channels, and bunding is repaired. If that could have been done with the Yellow River, we never would have suffered so much or so continually from floods. You know, I think, that the bed of the Yellow

River is high above the level of the country in many places, especially in Shantung, because the people kept building the dikes higher to keep pace with the silting of the bed of the river.

From the top of the Chengtu wall can be seen industrious people working everywhere. All the canals have mills working, mostly for grinding flour. The power is got by the swift water turning either vertical or horizontal water wheels. The water from the irrigation channels is served to all owners of fields through a complicated system which has been in force for centuries. Every field, or collection of fields, has its own level, differing a little from that of its neighbors, so that the water runs by gravity. Proper proportions of water are always available for every field without shortage or flooding. Famine is practically unknown because of this, and scarcity of food is rare.

In the city, as I have said, there is much manual industry. The streets are full of little shops which are also little factories, where everyone seems to be awfully busy making something or other — brassware, brushes from bristles, articles from horns, embroideries, and so on. Though for twenty years past the province has been disrupted by incessant civil wars signs of wealth are still abundant in Chengtu. In peaceful days of the past it must have been very rich. Gilded signs, now the worse for wear and neglect, still adorn many of the old shops. In the old days most of the travel in the city was done by better-off people in chairs fastened to the top curve of two long bent poles carried on the shoulders of coolies, with the curve upwards. Some of these chairs are still seen in the country. This type of chair enables the passenger to be kept above the heads of the throng. Now the motorcars traverse the streets to the annoyance of everyone but the people riding in them.

There are many schools and two universities at Chengtu, the foreign one being the West China Union University. The faculty of this university do a lot of excellent things to improve the lot and life of the people. They try to improve food supplies, and push the use of milk, introduce new varieties of plants, such as cabbages, corn, potatoes, and other vegetables.

When the weather got too hot we went to Omei Shan, the famous sacred mountain, some distance southwest of Chengtu. In the old days travelers had to go overland by chairs, or by junks down the Min River to near Kiating. We went by motorcar. We were able to realize how thickly populated was the Chengtu Plain, how rich the vegetation. Crops were lush — there is no other word for it. Waterways were spanned by strong bridges of great stone slabs. At each end of many bridges grew tremendous banyan trees, the widespreading branches of which sometimes met overhead and cast a shade over the whole bridge.

We had to cross the Min River — split into several branches, with islands of gravel between — by ferry or bridge. The ferry system was an ominous-looking affair, for the river was in flood and ran fast and furiously. Long cables held the barges carrying the motorcars, but we crossed the big stream in a junk and walked over the temporary bridges hung over the smaller waterways. The wildly rushing clear water was fascinating after seeing so much of the turbid streams of other parts of China.

When we came to this river we were met by a procession of boy scouts and girl guides. I was surprised to see them in this faraway part of western China, yet we encountered them everywhere. The boy scout uniform is now part and parcel of the student life of China, no matter how far, or in what direction, one may travel. I have seen them here in sight of the snow-clad mountains of Tibet, away in the northwest near the burning sands of the Gobi Desert, in the loess regions of Kansu, in the tropics of Yunnan, in remote Kweichow, and everywhere through the vast provinces from north to south China. They should have tremendous influence in time to come upon the character of our people, especially the illiterate ones.

After crossing the Min River the road wound through fertile country, with trees, sugar cane, rice fields, and many other things of interest. This part of our country has lots of moisture, both in the ground and in the air.

[129]

The clouds are so very much present that it is said the sun is obscured for such long periods that when it comes out the dogs are frightened of it and bark to chase it away. I wonder.

A long time before we got to Mount Omei we could see its bulky form rising high in the southwestern sky. It bursts upwards sheer out of the plain, or appears to do so. It is some 11,000 feet above sea level — a beautiful sight in the clear evening light. It looked like a huge headless animal crouching to spring. Its precipices are tremendous; straight walls of rock, some of which are said to be a mile high. I had no means of measuring them.

Once past the city of Omei Hsien, which we found clean and fresh, we felt that we were near our objective. We saw great banyan trees, and lots of white-branched trees encircling the paddy fields. I wondered if they were some relation to the white pines of north China, but later I learned that they were ash trees and that the white on the branches was wax deposited by insects. I was also told that this insect is peculiar to another part of the province and deposits the wax only on special trees. They had to be transported to this locality. However, it is an insect that contributes something definite to human economy, for the wax is treated and marketed.

We reached the bottom of the mountain, where the motor road ends, in time to be carried in chairs before darkness set in to the house in which we were to stay. We traveled alongside a torrential stream through a narrow tree-filled valley, the walls of which echoed and re-echoed to the vibrant screeching of thousands of cicadas. They seemed to be crying in chorus: "Free me; free me." I fervently wished that some magician would free me from them, for their unceasing stridulation tortured the very air. Unhappily there was no magician to waft me away—only the coolies who had no "waft" about them. They only puffed and blew as they climbed with me higher and higher toward the towering mountain. But we did not go up the mountain. We left the stone-paved pathway, with its innumerable steps, and ascended another which climbed over streams and through cornfields perched precariously on the sides of the steep hills. We were bound for a ridge about 4,000 feet above sea level on which some foreign-style houses had been built by missionaries to enable them to escape the terrible heat of the plains in summer.

There are many temples on the mountain, in all of which accommodation of a kind can be had, but the temples are noisy places, since they are also the inns for the pilgrims. The temples are not like the ornate structures of other parts of China. They are more like the great barns of the Swiss Alps. They are wooden-walled, heavy-thatched buildings without any adornment outside, and little inside. One section is set apart for the buddhas and for worship, but all the rest of the accommodation is for any travelers who come along. There are a few small rooms, but mostly the pilgrims hustle together in the large semiopen spaces. The noise they make by their conversations, by their arguments with chair carriers, and by their dickering with the priests, kills all possibility of sleep or rest, so the temples were not suitable for us. The heavy thatch is to keep out the constant heavy rain, and to bear the weight of the snow, for there is much snow on Omei Shan in the winter months. The buildings themselves are really huge caravanserais, and when the pilgrim seasons are on they need all their hugeness. Pilgrims come from all over China, and from distant places on the Tibetan border. The pathway up the mountain becomes a stream of puffing and perspiring human beings, most of whom climb the steps, women as well as men, as a penance.

We passed under two plum trees which were shedding their fruit to the delight of some peasants who were busily picking it up and putting it in baskets. Thick patches of bamboo jungle clung to the hillsides, and our pathway got steeper and steeper. Progress was very slow. On the hillsides were pine trees, and for a distance we saw the ash trees with the white insect wax, but after a certain height they did not appear again. There were thick growths of alder near the singing streams. Gorgeous butterflies were everywhere, making the ascent on upward currents of air. Thus these natural gliders reach the 11,000 feet summit.

We met several coolies carrying green shubbery. I could not understand why they were carrying so much green stuff down the steep trails. It looked to me at first like carting cement to Lungtan, but it suddenly dawned on me that they must be medicine plant gathers. I remembered that this part of Szechwan was in the most fertile region for such plants. I saw many of them in the days that followed. All had cloth wrapped round their legs like puttees; always they were soaking wet. They carried small machetes with which to cut or dig up the plants in the dense and dripping jungle.

The house we occupied was of weatherboard. Similar houses were scattered about at various distances. Far below us stretched the plain with the city of Kiating in the distance. The Min River glittered in the evening sunlight. A gorgeous panorama. We could see other cities, and lots and lots of villages. Another stream crossed the plain from the northwest to join the Min. Later on they were in flood, and communication with Omei by motorcar was stopped till a bridge could be repaired. Everywhere below us were farms and cultivation; everywhere above us were great bunches of cumulus cloud riding serenely to the moun-

[133]

tain crest, bumping and flowing over the top of the immense precipice like a waterfall at work upside down.

Later, I often saw the mountain solemnly purple in the sunshine; at times cloud-covered as if imitating a great iced cake. Some days it could not be seen at all. The ridge on which we lived had no level walking space. To go for a stroll one either went uphill or downhill. The growth on the hillsides was dense shubbery of sorts, and tangled bracken. There were some beautiful flowering plants. We used to climb to a little hillock where we could sit in the cool air and fading sunshine and gaze at the calm and aloof massiveness that is Omei Shan. On clear days the temple perched on the brink of the great precipice known as the Golden Summit was plainly visible. I used to wonder when I would get up there. I never managed it, I am sorry to say, but the Generalissimo went up with some others of the party. I can only tell you what they saw.

People who go to the top of Omei Shan want to see the snow-clad peaks of what they call Tibet. I suppose it is the Marches of Tibet, now named Sikong. I know that the white peaks do tower high toward the clouds there, for there are photographs of them. To see the peaks themselves one has to get up at daybreak on a fine morning and catch sight of them lightened up by the rosy glow of the rising sun. Later in the day the haze blots them out.

Another ambition of those who climb to the top is to

see the "Glory of Buddha." Clouds roll up so frequently that it is often seen. All that is required is a sunny day and that the clouds that float over the plain at a height of seven or ten thousand feet will drift to the great cliff and then stream up over it. If a person is standing on the cliff with the sun behind him his shadow will be projected on to the white cloud mass, and around the shadow will form a beautiful rainbow. The legend is that this phenomenon comes from the aureole of Buddha. The priests assert that it is a special symbol of the holiness of Omei Shan. It is said that some pilgrims are so moved by this that they leap over the cliff. A chain has been strung to iron posts to prevent people falling over, but they could still get over if they had a desire to tumble about a mile downward. There is another sight which pilgrims long to see — the lights that are said to float promiscuously in the air far below. Sceptics say they are the lanterns of woodsmen or farmers.

Near this spot stands a large bell, and some pieces of bronze; remains of what used to be a copper temple. It stood on the Golden Summit, the highest point of the mountain, until it was destroyed by fire caused by lightning in 1918. It is said to have been built by the Emperor Wan-li (1573-1620) and had many fine bronze panels, some of which are said to be beautifully designed, and valuable.

There are still two small bronze pagodas standing near the edge of the cliff, which reminds me that I forgot to tell you about the bronze pagoda at Kweiyang. That ornate and heavy piece of work, some twelve or more feet high, stands in a curiously shaped temple at the end of one of the bridges at Kweiyang. It remained there by accident. It was designed and made in Yunnan and destined for Peiping at the time of the Ming dynasty. It had to be carried over the mountains by hordes of coolies. By the time the coolies got it from Yunnan, over tremendous mountain ranges, to the approach of this bridge they became tired of carrying it. The mountains ahead were too much for them, so they abandoned it. The Kweiyangites built a temple around it, and thus came into possession of a relic that might have adorned one of the palaces at Peking and been a source of wonderment to millions of visitors. It now stands hidden far away in the middle of one of our remotest provinces and is seen by only the few travelers who pass there, if they are curious enough to enter the building to look at it.

When the bronze temple at Omei Shan burned, finis was written to it. No money could be found to rebuild it. I was told that the original one was bought by public subscription, a collection having been taken up all over China. I do not know what is the truth about it. The one thing certain is that it did exist, and the remains are there for anyone to see who has the strength to make the ascent.

To go to the top of Omei Shan from the bottom takes two days at least. The distance from where we used to sit and look at the massive front of the mountain seemed but fifteen miles. To walk the distance, however, one first had to descend about a thousand feet or more, then climb up five hundred or a thousand feet, descend again, and with such ups and downs still make progress upward. There are lots of temples on the way up. At the temple of the Flying Bridges there are two ways to go, one up the main paved path, or stairway, and the other along the bed of the torrent. That way passes through a narrow canyon which is traversed by way of a board staging which has been erected on beams set in holes on both sides of the canyon wall. The wood seemed pretty rotten to the party when they went up but none fell into the cold stream surging below. The path leads through gorges, and over hills, pine clad and profuse with flowers. Progress is a slow business, and tedious.

At intervals along the way there are stalls where food-stuffs of sorts are sold, as well as medicinal stuff, felspar, porcupine quills, deer horns and bones. I have seen some of these. They have herbs for every ailment, and the vendors seem to know what they are talking about. Carved staffs for the climbers are also sold. Everyone who walks or climbs must have a staff. And some of the staffs are unique. They are mostly of alder wood, carved with all manner of grotesque motives, depending upon what the shape of the root suggests — dragons, old men, women, serpents, and so on. Travelers like to take back a collection of them. At the Union University Museum at Chengtu I saw several which had been strikingly colored. One of our party made a collection but not being a careful person he lost it.

The priests on Omei are all Buddhists. There are a couple of thousand of them, I am told. The mountain is one of the four Buddhist sacred mountains of China, and the most distant, yet people are said to have tramped all the way to it from the coast to do penance.

The patron saint of the mountain is P'u-hsien Pu'ssa (Samantabhadra Bodhisattva), who is said to have descended on a great black elephant with six tusks. At Wannien-ssu temple there is a more than life-sized elephant in bronze. It was, according to records, carried up in pieces and then welded together. At this temple they also show what is alleged to be a tooth of Buddha. The only doubt about that story is that the so-called tooth is ten or twelve inches long and weighs several pounds. It looks, I am told, like the tooth of a dinosaur, or elephant. When the priest told one of our party that it was found farther up the mountain, he wanted to desert us at once to go and excavate for dinosaur remains and put the Gobi Desert discoveries in the shade.

Some distance farther up is the temple of the Elephant's Bath. What they show you for a bath is a cistern that no self-respecting elephant could get into, much less get out of. But I should think that particular temple would be more interesting to you children than any other for the apes that abound near there. They come to the terrace for food thrown to them by the pilgrims. One of the monks claims to be able to command the apes. They certainly come when he calls, screeching and chattering, hand over hand, through the branches of the trees — whole families of them. They travel right around the mountain about the same level above the sea, eating a dark-blue fruit. I suppose they find nuts of sorts, as well as chestnuts.

Most of the temples have been built on commanding sites, and are picturesquely located. One of the most pleasing is said to be that near the cave of the Immortals. This cave goes some distance into the mountain, and the believing are sure that it connects Omei Shan with Kiangsi Province, or some other equally distant place. The Immortals are said to have traveled on foot through the cave to Omei Shan. The cave is now the home of thousands of bats—who cling to each other until they form large living clusters far away in the dark—and of swarms of swallows who have covered the walls and sides of the cave with their gray mud nests.

Seeing that swallows do not have flashlights and do not have numbers painted on their doors, how do Mr. and Mrs. Swallow find their way home? And how do the baby swallows, flying in the blackness, find out which of the thousands of closely packed nests is theirs? None of our party was courageous enough to try to walk back to wherever the other end of the cave is supposed to be, all those who went in being content to turn back when the walls narrowed and the smell became too overpowering. Some distance inside they found a shrine, and a bubbling spring of cold water. The mouth of the cave opened out high up on a steep mountainside. A track was cut to it by the priests so that the pilgrims might see the way the Immortals came to the mountain.

Large trees grow profusely here. Much silver fir is seen. That tree provides the timber for the temples. There are groves near the top of the mountain, many standing stark and splintered, having been struck by lightning. Thunderstorms are frequent on this peak, the reverberations of the thunder roaring round the great precipices and through the gorges and chasms in a terrifying manner.

Hydrangea and rhododendrons are prevalent. So are berries — raspberry and blackberry. One spot is famous

for its white strawberries. They are said to be much sought
after by the pilgrims who have grown thirsty climbing
the steep steps. These strawberries grow on a thickly
wooded tableland, the edges of which are sheer precipices.
Wonderful views are to be had of the ridges and valleys
lying far below, which nurse clouds of all grotesque and
picturesque formations, and of the distant plain stretching far away in all directions. To get this view in safety
paths have been cut in one or two places through the
thick shrubbery and ferns.

The climb up Omei Shan is a terrific business. There
are innumerable steps for weary legs to tremble over, since
chairs cannot be carried up them. That is why I did not
try to go up this time. Chairs can be used most of the
distance along one line of ascent, but on the other—the
one that passes the temple of the Immortals—the steps are
dizzily dangerous, and numerous.

There is one method of riding that is interesting, but
not to my taste. I saw several aged women using it. The
coolie straps to his back a frame of wood which has a kind
of seat. The passenger straddles this, hangs on to the
coolie's head, and appears to be riding pickaback. It is a
good way for the elderly to go up and down the veritable
ladders, if they keep their eyes shut, and at the same time
it is the cheapest form of conveyance. Some of the elderly
pilgrims ride in that fashion from bottom to top and back

again. Merit is always achieved by getting to the top of Omei, no matter how one gets there, though to crawl up on one's knees is the best way of acquiring forgiveness for sins. But it must hurt the knees, I can hear you say. No matter which way one goes up some part of one's anatomy will ultimately ache, but one of these days I shall try the ascent, and then I shall tell you more about it. Just now I think this is enough. When you grow up you will be able, perhaps, to climb the famous mountain yourselves.

2.

THE OLD ORDER CHANGETH

"No other country on the face of the earth has stepped so quickly out of the Middle Ages into the twentieth century."

I HAD accompanied my husband to Fukien. On Christmas Day we traveled over one thousand li (333 miles) partly by air and partly by the new military road he had built after the Fukien trouble started. We arrived at Puchen, over the Fukien border, after two hours in the air and eight hours by motorcar from Hangchow. During that time we had crossed the boundaries of Chekiang, Kiangsi, and Fukien provinces, and I was so weary from being jolted and bumped over the rough roads through the most mountainous part of eastern China that I could scarcely hold up my head.

In spite of my weariness I marveled at the scenery. It was gorgeous, unlike anything I have ever seen. I know the American Rockies. They are rugged and majestic. But Fukien has range upon range of mountains covered with delectable foliage, thousands upon thousands of fir trees in their Christmas green, brightened here and there, in startling contrast, by a single candleberry tree of flaming red. To think that a road had been built through this mountainous region within a month's time! Considering the topography of the region and the rapidity of accomplishment, experts regard it as a Herculean task. Whole sides of mountains were cut through by hand labor. To be sure, thousands of men were employed, working in three shifts. It was also a rough country road. But it was there.

Sometimes the road passed through a cut so narrow and deep that the mountains seemed ready to topple over on us. I thought of the pass of Thermopylae and wondered if it was like this. Again we motored along the edge of a plateau where the least swerve would have flung us over the precipice. Parts of the highway were still under construction, and the steep gradings seemed almost perpendicular. It was not until we had reached our journey's end that I realized how dangerous the trip had been and how great the strain. Then my husband began to reproach himself for submitting me to such hazards. Fortunately, in times of actual danger one does not feel so acutely as in retrospect.

To illustrate this, I am reminded of an incident which occurred at field headquarters in Kiangsi recently [1] in the dead of night. Suddenly we heard the crack, crack, crack of several hundred shots from the direction of the city

[1] This was written in 1934.

wall. What had happened? The General was up instantly, calling me to dress hurriedly. He ordered the secret-service men to investigate. The shots became more frequent, more insistent. Shivering with cold, in the feeble candle-light I threw on my clothes and sorted out certain papers which must not fall into enemy hands. I kept them within reach to be burnt if we had to leave the house. Then I took my revolver and sat down to wait for what might come. I heard my husband giving orders for all available guards to form a cordon, so that we could shoot our way out if we were actually surrounded.

We did not yet know what was happening outside but we did know that the enemy had been close pressed lately and was desperate. After an hour, reports came back that a portion of the enemy troops had staged a surprise attack under cover of darkness, knowing that only a few hundred sentries guarded the city wall. While we were in apparent danger I was not frightened. I had only two things on my mind: the papers giving information of our troop positions and movements and the determination, should I be taken captive, to shoot myself. I would prefer death to the fate of women who fall into the hands of bandits. But, fortunately, the attack was repelled, and we went back to sleep.

A month later we were in Puchen, within the borders of the province to the south. Isolated little city! Until the

road I have described was built, the city had little communication with the outside world. Devious footpaths
through almost impassable mountains did not encourage
travel. The people belonged to another age. I saw there
costumes like those of my great-grandmother and the
elaborate hairdressing of a century ago.

On New Year's Eve, my husband and I took a walk in
the surrounding mountains. We discovered a tree of white
plum blossoms, flowering profusely. What an omen of
good luck ! In Chinese literature the five petals of the
winter plum portend the five blessings of joy, good luck,
longevity, prosperity, and (to us most desired of all) peace!
The General carefully plucked a few branches and carried them home. When our evening candles were lighted,
he presented them to me in a little bamboo basket — a
New Year's gift. The plum blossoms had looked graceful
and lovely on the tree, but massed in the basket by candle-
light they took on an indescribable beauty, their shadows
on the wall making clean, bold strokes like those of the
great Ming artist, Pah Dah Shan Jen. Perhaps you can
see why I am willing to share the rigors of life at the front
with my husband. He has the courage of the soldier and
the sensitive soul of the poet.

At the end of a week my husband left for Kien-Or, a
point farther south. It took him only an hour by military
plane, but the trip was bitterly cold and hazardous, so he

wired me to proceed by sampan. Do you know what a sampan is like? Twenty feet long by six feet wide, it is a shallow-bottomed boat, usually propelled by two boatmen, with room for two or three passengers in the covered mid-section. I had with me my American nurse, my woman secretary, an amah, men servants, and guards. Since we numbered altogether about sixty or seventy, we had five sampans and five bamboo rafts.

The bamboo raft, too, is an interesting invention. Made of eight thick bamboo poles tied together with bamboo peel, it resembles nothing so much as a huge toboggan sled. The likeness is increased by the fact that the front end of the raft is heated until pliable and then bent upward, curving gradually to an angle of forty-five degrees, so that it can take the water smoothly and rapidly.

The rivers of Fukien have rapids in places, and water so shallow in others that the trip is full of exciting moments. Through shallow waters the boatmen pole the sampans from rock to rock or push them along the shore with bamboo poles steel spiked at the ends. So frequently did we scrape the rocks or hit against the boulders of the rapids that one of the boats burst open against a sharp jagged rock, splitting its sides. My sampan sprang a leak, but the damage was less serious. At that we were kept busy bailing out the water and stuffing the hole with absorbent cotton.

[147]

These little boats have a bamboo-matting cover amid-ships. At night, by rigging up padded cotton curtains, it is like a little cabin with some degree of privacy. During the day, however, this little room must be kept open at both ends so that the boatmen can look ahead or behind as they pole the boat. For my bed some planks were laid along one side, on which a mattress was placed. I used this narrow berth for bed by night and seat by day. The other three women had to spread their bedding in the bottom of the boat.

Our quarters were cramped enough, but we felt safer together. Though the guards stood on duty, our boats had to tie up during the night in the bandit-infested country. In the early evening we would restore warmth to our half-frozen bodies by gathering rushes and making huge bon-fires on the rocky bank, where we thawed out tingling toes. The glow warmed our hearts as well and lit up the whole countryside. We were not unaware that the bonfire might attract unwelcome attention to our party, but en-countering bandits seemed the lesser evil as compared with frost and hunger pangs.

The two boatmen in our sampan were brothers, the younger an engaging youth of nineteen. He beamed and sang more lustily each day to please me. These two had a tune, the younger asking a question in a sort of chant, the other replying antiphonally. For example, when we came to a bend in the river, the younger would sing: "Hey ho, how is the wa-water cur-ur-urr-ving, hey ho ?"

And the older at the front of the boat would respond: "Yay ho ya, ho, a-a-a-ll ri-i-ight, bu-but kee-eep stead-yyy, yay he, ya ho!"

Then when they came to a particularly difficult place they would heave to with all their strength while chanting in unison, "Ya ho, he, ho, careful !"

The first night we moored near the home of these two boatmen. When we made camp they came to me and said, "Tai-tai (Respected Lady), will you and all your party honor us at the evening meal?" Considering that besides rice the only food they would have for supper probably was that which they held in their hands—a bunch of green onions and a pound of pork—how could I accept their invitation? I finally pleaded fatigue but promised to send an aide-de-camp to thank them after supper. Thus was the situation saved. They had not lost face, and I had not failed in courtesy.

The distance my husband flew in less than an hour took four days and nights by small boat. Toward the last lap of this journey we passed through areas still actively infested with scattered bands of roving bandits. The General sent additional guards to meet us. Fortunately, we met with no mishap. At night, however, I could scarcely sleep, haunted as I was by the deserted farms and ravaged villages I had seen during the day. After being cramped for hours in the sampan I would frequently get out and cut across the hills on foot, rejoining our little fleet several miles beyond. Desirous of not attracting attention, I would take only two or three plain-clothes men with me and leave the other guards behind.

On these walks I passed through many villages, often completely deserted. Sometimes there would be a little life. More often they were dead to all intents and purposes, for I could not find a single human being or animal in sight. Silence, like a thick pall, hung over the empty houses. The only sound in all the village was the tap, tap of my walking stick and the pad of our footsteps on the cobblestones of the one long street. Vacant houses stood with doors gaping wide. Inside mutilated pieces of furniture sprawled in confusion. The walls were scorched and blackened from hurried attempts to destroy them, mute testimony to the relentless fury of the marauders.

Everything that could not be carried away had been damaged. Devastation and death silently pervaded the whole hamlet. A Chinese village is normally full of life, movement, and rhythm—the cries of hawkers, the laughter of children, the good-natured jostling of people in the street, the grunting of pigs running at large. But here not even a lean dog was in sight. Emptiness, desolation, desertion. Why? Bandits.

I hurried into the open fields. I could not bear to linger in the village. But again! Instead of what were once swaying fields of golden grain, I found here a stubble of blackened roots, there a heap of broken tiles, and, beyond, barren wasteland. The tiller of the soil may have been killed. If lucky, he may have escaped with a hen tucked under each arm, a bundle of bedding on his back, and wife and children following at his heels with a few earthen pots and bowls.

The next day the motion of the swaying sampan made me seasick, and again I walked. We passed through a village where a few old men were basking in the sun.

"Where are the people of the village?" I asked.

They continued to gaze into space. At long last one answered listlessly:

"The bandits have been here!"

Then after another silence, as though loath to speak:

"Some of the people have been killed. Some were carried away. Some escaped, heaven knows where! We were too old and weary, so we hid beneath the straw and we are left."

They alone were there to tell the tale.

Later that same day I was walking alone when I heard a guard say, as I passed a camphor tree:

"What a wonderful coffin that would make!"

In any other country the remark would have seemed

incongruous, a superficial comment in a spirit of levity. Not so in China. The Chinese coffin cut from huge slabs of wood, the more massive the better, is literally a longevity article. If presented to the ill it will propitiate the spirits. If prepared for the aged it assures a feeling of peace and tranquillity.

Just at that moment I stubbed my toe. Over what? A piece of ancient crème glacée perhaps? When the Nanking airdrome was built a few years ago, antiques were dug up, some of them a thousand years old. They are now in the provincial museum. Perhaps I had stumbled on some such antique. I stooped to see. It was almost an antique but it was not a vase. It was a human skull.

Victory was ours in less than two months in Fukien, partly because of modern aviation. Victory is in sight in Kiangsi as I write. But when the rebellious army has been brought to terms and the bandits have been forced from their mountainous strongholds, that is not the end of the problem. A long, slow process of rural rehabilitation must be undertaken if the people who have lost land and property and farm animals and household possessions (meager as they were) and gallant spirit are to be enabled to carry on again in the fundamentally important task of wrestling a livelihood from mother earth. In this task the government and all philanthropic organizations are co-operating. Experts are working with us on this rehabilitation program, and we are pushing ahead in a glorious enterprise. It will not make front-page news but it will mean a contented peasantry. The army has done its part. Modern aviation has immeasurably facilitated its success. Now comes a long, steady pull. Where a nation's people are contented, seeds of so destructive a type of banditry as we have seen in China do not readily take root.

Section V

MY FAITH

I.

WHAT RELIGION
MEANS TO ME

"With me religion is a very simple thing. It means to try with all my heart and soul and strength and mind to do the will of God."

By nature I am not a religious person. At least not in the common acceptance of that term. I am not by nature a mystic. I am practical-minded. Mundane things have meant much to me, perhaps too much. Mundane, not material, things. I care more for a beautiful celadon vase than for costly jewels. I am more disturbed by travel through the crowded, dirty streets of an interior city than I am by the hazards of flying with poor visibility. Personal danger means nothing to me. But I am concerned that my school for the children of the revolutionary heroes shall raise for them, and perhaps for the communities to which they return, the standard of living and the quality of life.

Also, I am more or less skeptical. I used to think Faith, Belief, Immortality were more or less imaginary. I believed

[157]

in the world seen, not the world unseen. I could not accept
things just because they had always been accepted. In
other words, a religion good enough for my father did not
necessarily appeal to me. I do not yet believe in predigested
religion in palatable, sugar-coated doses.

I knew my mother lived very close to God. I recognized
something great in her. And I believe that my childhood
training influenced me greatly even though I was more or
less rebellious at the time. It must often have grieved my
beloved mother that I found family prayers tiresome and
frequently found myself conveniently thirsty at the moment, so that I had to slip out of the room. Like my
brothers and sisters, I always had to go to church and I
hated the long sermons. But today I feel that this church-
going habit established something, a kind of stability,
for which I am grateful to my parents.

My mother was not a sentimental parent. In many
ways she was Spartan. But one of my strongest childhood
impressions is of mother going to a room she kept for the
purpose on the third floor to pray. She spent hours in prayer, often beginning before dawn. When we asked her ad-
vice about anything, she would say, "I must ask God
first." And we could not hurry her. Asking God was not
a matter of spending five minutes to ask Him to bless her
child and grant the request. It meant waiting upon God
until she felt His leading. And I must say that whenever

mother prayed and trusted God for her decision, the undertaking invariably turned out well.

Perhaps this is why I sometimes think that I have grown spiritually because mother was taken from me. Or, to be perfectly honest, I sometimes think perhaps God took mother from her children in order that we might grow. As long as mother lived I had a feeling that whatever I did, or failed to do, mother would pray me through. Though she insisted that she was not our intercessor, that we must pray ourselves, yet I know for a certainty that many of her long hours of prayer were spent interceding for us. Perhaps it is because religion in my mind is associated with such a mother that I have never been able to turn away from it entirely.

Before I leave the subject of prayer, I want to tell you of a lesson I learned from my mother. It was shortly before she left us. She was ill and already confined to her bed. Japan had begun to show her hand in Manchuria. Most of this we kept from mother. One day I was talking with her about the imminent Japanese menace and I suddenly cried out in irresistible intensity of feeling:

"Mother, you're so powerful in prayer. Why don't you pray that God will annihilate Japan — by an earthquake or something?"

She turned her face away for a time. Then looking gravely at me she said: "When you pray, or expect me to pray, don't insult God's intelligence by asking Him to do something which would be unworthy even of you, a mortal!"

That made a deep impression on me. And today I can pray for the Japanese people, knowing that there must be many, who, like Kagawa, suffer because of what their country is doing to China.

During the past years I have suffered much. I have gone through deep waters because of the chaotic conditions in China: the lopping off of our richest provinces, the death of my saintly mother, flood, famine, and the intrigues of those who should have been helping to unify the country. All these things have made me see my own inadequacy. More than that, all human insufficiency. To try to do anything for the country seemed like trying to put out a great conflagration with a cup of water. In contemplating history I began to feel the futility of life. Sometimes I would say to myself (never to my husband): "What if we do achieve a strong, unified country? In the sum total of things what does it amount to? As surely as a country rises to its zenith, so surely does it decline!"

During these years of my married life, I have gone through three phases as related to my religion. First, there was a tremendous enthusiasm and patriotism — a passionate desire to do something for my country. Here was my opportunity. With my husband, I would work ceaseless-

ly to make China strong. I had the best of intentions, but
something was lacking. There was no staying power. I
was depending on self.

Then came the second phase. These things that I have
referred to happened, and I was plunged into dark despair. A terrible depression settled on me — spiritual
despair, bleakness, desolation. At the time of my mother's
death the blackness was greatest. A foreign foe was on our
soil in the north. A discontented political faction in the
south. Famine in the northwest. Floods threatening the
millions who dwell in the Yangtze valley. And my beloved
mother taken from us. What was left?

And then I realized that spiritually I was failing my
husband. My mother's influence on the General had been
tremendous. His own mother was a devout Buddhist. It
was my mother's influence and personal example that led
him to become a Christian. Too honest to promise to be
one just to win her consent to our marriage, he had promised my mother that he would study Christianity and read
the Bible. And I suddenly realized that he was sticking to
his promise, even after she was gone, but losing spiritually
because there were so many things he did not understand.
In common parlance, I have to "hand it to him" for sticking to his daily Old Testament reading when without il-
lumination there was little help in it for him.

I began to see that what I was doing to help, for the

sake of the country, was only a substitute for what he needed. I was letting him head toward a mirage when I knew of the oasis. Life was all confusion. I had been in the depths of despair. Out of that, and the feeling of human inadequacy, I was driven back to my mother's God. I knew there was a power greater than myself. I knew God was there. But mother was no longer here to help the General spiritually, and in helping him I grew spiritually myself.

Thus I entered into the third period, where I wanted to do not my will, but God's. Life is really simple, and yet how confused we make it. In old Chinese art, there is just one outstanding object, perhaps a flower, on a scroll. Everything else in the picture is subordinate to that one beautiful thing. An integrated life is like that. What is that one flower? As I feel it now, it is the will of God. But to know His will, and do it, calls for absolute sincerity and honesty. Political life is full of falsity and diplomacy and expediency. My firm conviction is that one's greatest weapon is not more deceptive falsity, more subtle diplomacy, greater expediency, but the simple, unassailable weapons of sincerity and truth.

Solomon showed his greatness when he asked God not for wealth or fame or power, but for wisdom — for the sake of his country. It is nothing just to be good. That can be read backwards — good for nothing. One must have moral conviction, wisdom, and the energy to accomplish. I used to pray that God would do this or that. Now I pray only that God will make His will known to me. God speaks to me in prayer. Prayer is not self-hypnotism, it is more than meditation. The Buddhist priests spend days meditating. In meditation the source of strength is oneself. But when one prays he goes to a source of strength greater than his own. I wait to feel His leading, and His guidance means certainty.

In the feudal time of the Three Kingdoms, there was an old general called Ts'ao Ts'ao. Once upon a time he was going on a long march. His soldiers were weary, thirsty, discouraged. He said to them, "From my horse I can see a beautiful garden, full of luscious plums!" Their mouths watered, new strength and courage came to them. But for how long? The plum garden did not materialize, and the soldiers were more weary than before. That to me is like meditation. There is a buoyancy of spirit for a time. It may help when there is no oasis in sight. But when I am spiritually thirsty I do not think of plum gardens — I go to the fountain of living water.

There are two things in the Bible that impress me more than others. One is, "Thy will be done," and the other, "Thou shalt love the Lord, thy God, with all thy heart and with all thy soul and with all thy strength and with all thy mind." We have to use our minds as well as our hearts. The road to hell is paved with good intentions. And I know of nothing more aggravating than a well-meaning person who has no judgment. Prayer is our source of guidance and balance. God is able to enlighten the understanding. I am often bewildered, because my mind is only finite. I question and doubt my own judgments. Then I seek guidance, and when I am sure I go ahead, leaving the results with Him.

Our finite minds beside His infinite mind seem to me like this: I go walking, and the hills loom above me, range upon range, one against the other. I cannot tell where one begins and another leaves off. But from the air (I seldom have time to travel any other way now) everything has a distinct contour and form. I can see things so much more clearly. Perhaps that is like my mind and God's. And when I talk with Him, He lifts me up where I can see clearly.

I do not think it is possible to make this understandable to one who has not tried it. To explain what it means to one who has had no experience of getting guidance would be like trying to make a stone-deaf person understand the beauty of a Chopin sonata. A physicist or a specialist in tones and their wave lengths might convey some idea of it to such an one. I do not know. But I'm sure I could not.

What I do want to make clear is that, whether we get guidance or not, it is there. It's like tuning in on the radio.

MY FAITH

There is music in the air, whether we tune in or not. By learning to tune in, we can understand. How is it done? As Brother Lawrence told us long ago, "by practicing the presence of God." By daily communion with Him. One cannot expect to be conscious of God's presence when one has only a bowing acquaintance with Him.

In conclusion, with me religion is a very simple thing. It means to try with all my heart and soul and strength and mind to do the will of God. I feel that God has given me a work to do for China. China's problems in some ways are greater today than ever before. But despondency and despair are not mine. I look to Him who is able to do all things, even more than we ask or think.

2.

CHRISTIANITY IN AN
AWAKENED CHINA

"The new China will arise upon founda-
tions already laid by our ancestors, and
not upon the current 'isms' of our age."

ONE thing that society asks of the church is that it shall
show men how to meet the pressing problems of their day.
In the midst of a poisoned social atmosphere a strong religious faith should act not merely as a gas mask to protect
its wearer, but it should also be as a cleansing breeze that
gradually changes and purifies the dwelling places of
men.

The church can no longer stand apart from the development of modern China. The whole of the Chinese nation is on the march. The church must march with it.
Beacon after beacon is being lighted across the country,
warning the people that they must arise to attack the
strongly entrenched social evils of our day, and to help
usher in the new order of things. The bugle call of the

New Life Movement is sounding clearly in the dawn of China's new day.

One critic of the New Life Movement has said that the real question of the masses is one of livelihood, and the New Life Movement has done nothing about it. I want to pass that challenge on.

In the summer of 1933 I received an invitation to join a discussion group at Kuling on the subject of Christians and communism. At that time I found Christians willing to discuss these problems of livelihood in a rather academic way, and I became convinced that somehow we should be more practical in the application of our faith. The National Christian Council later co-operated with the government in organizing eleven rural experiment centers in Kiangsi where young men and women from Christian and other colleges might take the lead in studying and trying to solve some of the most pressing needs of the farmers. It has been a source of great satisfaction to the Generalissimo and myself that the church has united with us in the rehabilitation of recovered bandit areas. We hope this is merely a beginning in this great field of improving the life of the people.

Perhaps one reason why the church has been slow to engage in this work of rural reconstruction is on account of the hardships involved. At such a time as this we should honestly face the fact that we have not accustomed ourselves to enduring hardships as good soldiers of Jesus Christ. In this we are weak. In the words of the Prophet, "Woe to them that are at ease in Zion."

As my husband and I have traveled over many provinces we have met devoted missionaries, living far away in the interior, bringing new life to the communities that they touch. We have been astonished at the absence of talented modern-educated Chinese men and women, either supporting these heroic missionaries, or carrying on similar activities in like needy areas. Is it possible that modern trained Chinese Christians lack the stuff of which missionaries are made? Are we in the position of accepting all the benefits of the Christian faith without caring to accept the responsibilities and the hardships?

At the very heart of our faith is hardship, endurance, suffering — a cross. Without them there cannot be any Christian faith. I have frequently heard the Generalissimo remark that Christ, as a young man, willingly gave up his life for the cause, and that we shall not be able to solve our own great problems until more of us are ready to do likewise. That is why he feels that Christianity is a revolutionary faith, and that every man of faith in such a world as ours should be a revolutionary.

In this age of grim necessity, when the utmost qualities of men and of nations are on trial, to have a robust Christian faith means that we will never give in. This age will be changed in the proportion that our faith, personality, and enthusiasm soak into it. Just as we deduce the value of medicine from its effects, so we appraise the quality of our faith from its moral effect upon ourselves and upon society.

What we need today is to feel certain about the call of God and to make some decisions at the price of our comfort and, if need be, of our necks. Perception and action must go together. We are called to translate our faith into the life of our day.

Like the Sleeping Beauty in the castle, surrounded by high hedges of thorns, China has at last been awakened to live in a new and wonderful world of progress. In this new world the church has a large place to fill, provided it is willing to move forward and to endure.

One singular thing about our Christian faith is that it is not merely a social creed, but a revelation from God. There is no such thing as revelation of itself, for revelation consists always of the fact that something is revealed to us. In our day God is revealing Himself anew in the needs of society, and impressing upon us the need for social action on our part. Let the younger churches of the East, and the older churches of the West, unite in a grand effort to bring New Life to the people of the towns and the villages. As in response to the season the trees have borne their fruit and the fields their grain, so the New

China has responded to seasonable co-operation from the churches of the West.

One of the outstanding examples of co-operation between church and government is to be found in Kiangsi. Not merely the Lichwan experiment, but ten other welfare centers have been organized under the leadership of Mr. Chang Fu-liang, the National Christian Council Rural Secretary. Visitors have often remarked that they see little difference between Lichwan and the other ten centers, now under the Ministry of Industry. How could there be any difference when they all embody the same Christian ideals of service, and have the same leadership?

Neither in Lichwan, nor in the ten other welfare centers, have we attempted to reconstruct rural life in a way that is peculiar to Christians. Rather, we have attempted to discover methods that may be readily used by anyone interested in the welfare of the people.

The church has demonstrated that it is willing to lend some of its men for work in this vast field of rural reconstruction the edge of which we have scarcely touched. The Kingdom of God is real indeed when it can be brought down to life in the village of war-torn Kiangsi.

Yet another place where church and government have been developing co-operation is in the health plans for the nation. The first public health body in China, the Council on Health Education, was carried on for years under Christian auspices. Now that its functions have been largely taken over by the government there are many gaps in the national health program that mission and church hospitals can fill. I am glad to know that the National Christian Council has a medical secretary assigned to this work of co-operation.

Some time ago the Central Health Administration at Nanking had 40,000 dozen tubes of smallpox vaccine available for use in country districts. The New Life Movement was appealed to, through its medical adviser, Mrs. Shepherd, and she immediately arranged with local New Life Movement associations in a few of the provinces to co-operate with mission hospitals, schools, and country churches in conducting vaccination campaigns in near-by villages. Health authorities have not yet perfected their machinery for reaching all the neglected areas, and, until they have, here is one place where the church is still able to serve the people. One-fourth of the available vaccine has been applied for, and is now being distributed. Sixty thousand people are being vaccinated through the combined efforts of government health stations, New Life Movement associations, hospitals, schools, and churches.

In Canton a Women's Prayer League of a thousand members is being formed, all of whom pledge themselves and their families to pray daily for China and her leaders. This is one of the most practical forms of patriotism and one that will go far toward bringing about a strong spiritual unity.

Such co-operation need not overconcern itself with correct doctrines and pious aspirations, but with China's ancient heritage, with sacrifice, and with love for our fellows in His name.

Christianity has been correctly styled as materialistic, because in Christian lands have developed most of the modern scientific inventions which today go to make life longer and more comfortable. Other nations, such as ancient Greece, have given us the elements of physical science, but only in Christian countries have these sciences fully developed and become the common possession of all. In China we are rapidly introducing these modern ways of living to our people, and they are accepting them without question. The Apostle Paul dignified the whole physical life of man when he said, "Know ye not that your body is the temple of the Holy Spirit. . .?" A more comfortable physical life is desirable for all, and not merely for the privileged few. Surely it is one of the responsibilities of the followers of Christ to see that "New Life" is put within the reach of all.

The status of women has been raised wherever the Christian faith has become known. Not so long ago, mission schools in China had to offer girls free tuition and spending money to induce them to accept a modern education. It is to the lasting credit of the missionaries that they used every means to get girls to study. Now these trained women are at the heart of many of the movements working to improve the living conditions and the status of their sisters throughout the provinces. Their faith is already in action. Let us carry our co-operative program, between New Life and the churches, for the improvement of the life of women and children, into every village and hamlet throughout the land. The Christian Church throughout the world is rich in finances and in consecrated enthusiastic youth. Let us concentrate some of these resources upon the great need of our day.

There are always those, even among our own people, who are afraid that co-operation with the government will not succeed. In Nanchang a prominent church social worker was severely criticized by her own group for spending so much time and energy co-operating with the Women's New Life Committee of the Provincial Government. We oftentimes lose sight of the fact that, through well-thought-out co-operation and service, everybody benefits. The church stands to benefit most of all from an enlightened, prosperous community, and in my opinion no enlightened community can afford to be without a church.

MY FAITH

Many educational institutions under the direction of Christians have contributed greatly toward bringing New Life to thousands of students. The low cost of administration and the high quality of work in Christian schools, often maintained under difficult circumstances, have all left their mark upon the nation. In the matter of education let us not "grow weary in well doing" and give up our work just half completed. The Generalissimo and I both feel that a religious faith is essential to a well-rounded life. Without it education is incomplete. The nation is in great need of leaders, in all walks of life, who have Christian ideals of service and live up to them.

The Y.M.C.A. and the Y.W.C.A. have been in the front line of leadership and have slowly, through the years, been pressing upon us the necessity of a change in our manner of living. These two associations are considered one of our greatest aids in giving youth a zest for New Life.

We must constantly remind ourselves that Jesus' respect for personality did not stop with an interest in individuals. He was deeply concerned with the welfare of society, and talked incessantly about the Kingdom of Heaven, wherein dwell righteousness and justice for all.

The Chinese people have always displayed a profound respect for personality and have been severely criticized by visitors for giving much time and thought to courtesy and "face." Much of life is regulated by the requirements of custom, and the necessity for maintaining dignity. Offense must not be given, wherever it can be avoided. The ideal society, according to the genius of our race, is the "Golden Mean," the middle of the road. All manners of extremes are to be avoided.

The totalitarian state will not meet with much response in China as long as it continues to exalt the state at the expense of the individual and to crush personality in its fanatical drive toward establishing authority. The New Life Movement has definitely rejected all forms of regimentation as being opposed to the principles of Dr. Sun Yat-sen and as betraying the Chinese people into the hands of those who, in their innermost souls, do not respect personality or the rights of individuals and groups.

The Chinese people have always had a mind of their own and will continue to think for themselves. They can co-operate only with those who understand their culture, their sense of justice, and their love of freedom. Chinese society has within itself the germ of a new life, but it needs direction and a deeper religious faith. The new China will arise upon foundations already laid by our ancestors, and not upon the current "isms" of our age.

Because of the trend of world events in some circles

there is a tendency toward discouragement, but our Christian faith will cease to be faith when we can no longer believe in the regeneration of a nation. The primary interest of Christianity is not systematic knowledge, known as theology, nor yet philosophy, though it may include these, but the relation of a personal faith to the men and women around us. One thing we must do is to find the point of contact between our faith and contemporary life. The need of our times should determine our perspective.

God, who all down through history has spoken to men through revelation, can through His Holy Spirit speak to us here. When He speaks we will know, for it will both convince the mind and satisfy the heart. In discovering the need for regeneration, and the resources at hand for meeting this need, we shall be drawn and carried along as on the crest of a great wave. As we proceed, the details of our task will be made clear and comprehensive.

Two striking things about Christ are that he lived what he preached, and he had faith that could remove mountains. We shall need both these qualities in increasing measure if we are to carry through this breath-taking venture of pointing the way to a new social order. The New Life Movement asks us to live up to the highest principles known to man, and to move forward in faith. Both call for positive action on the part of individuals and society, and are well within the realm of our Christian experience.

With reference to the regeneration of the nation, as I have intimated, important changes in the life of the people of China must come within the system given to us by our late leader, Dr. Sun Yat-sen. The founder of the Chinese Republic was a man of faith and action. He had within his soul a burning passion for the uplift of the people who toil. Beyond the slightest trace of doubt, he walked in the steps of the Master. He lived in faith, and died in faith, leaving to us the task of completing the more important stages of the revolution.

The most important factor in reconstruction is the spiritual renewal of the people and the improvement of their character. We cannot create the social life of the people, history has a long start on us in that, but it is within our power to regenerate it, and wholly transform it by breathing into it a new soul.

The beginning of the Christian life is really a "radical and permanent moral change wrought in the spiritual nature," and commonly referred to as the New Birth. "A change in the growing purpose, reformation of habits and life, and continuation by the Holy Spirit of new ways of living," is New Life from within and the right place to begin the regeneration of a nation. In a large measure this part of reconstruction is pre-eminently the work of the church. Then let us do it together, the New Life Movement and the church.

Section VI

A TALE OF OLD CHINA

LITTLE SISTER SU

*"Her gestures suggest willow leaves
in the breeze, and her movements
bespeak delicacy and precision."*

DURING the Sung dynasty, when the Chinese essay form
reached a degree of literary perfection never since equaled,
there lived in the province of Szechwan an old scholar
named Su-Hsin. Since he had received no schooling what-
soever up to the age of twenty-seven, it was all the more
remarkable that he finally attained literary eminence and
became a member of the Han-lin Yuan, the Imperial
Academy, whose members were the most distinguished
scholars of the country.

Su had two sons and a young daughter. The sons also
ranked among the well-known essayists of the period. To
distinguish them from their father and from each other,
the father was known as Old Su, the elder son Big Su, and
the younger one Little Su. The writings of the trio survive to the present day. Those of Big Su rank among the
classics; their exquisite rhythm and inimitable style are
the despair of ambitious imitators.

Although Old Su was proud of his sons, he loved most
of all his daughter, whom the family affectionately called

[183]

Little Sister. He gave her the same education he had given her brothers; and, since she possessed natural literary gifts, she became wonderfully proficient and at the age of sixteen outshone scholars many years her senior. Her unusual intellectual attainments gave her father as much anxiety as pleasure, however, for he feared it would be difficult to find a husband sufficiently brilliant to please her.

One day the Premier, Wang An-shih, invited Su-Hsin to dinner. Old Su detested the Premier heartily. He had written satires attacking Wang for promoting queer and freakish fads in order to draw public attention to himself. But for the sake of expediency he accepted the invitation. The Premier disliked Old Su as cordially, but he thought it wise to maintain a semblance of friendship with the literary trio, the biting sting of whose wit he had felt on more than one occasion.

Dinner ended, Old Su and the Premier sat in the library. In cup after cup of wine they challenged each other. His tongue loosened by the strong drink, the Premier boasted of his son's literary talents.

"My sons, too, are no mean writers," retorted Old Su, equally flushed with wine. "Besides, my daughter. . ."

"Oh, daughters!" rudely interrupted the half-drunken Premier. "Ha, ha, ten candles are not to be compared with one lamp," he laughed, quoting a proverb.

"Were there no daughters, there could be no mothers,"

said Old Su, rebuking him with considerable heat, and also quoting a proverb.

"Mm, mm," continued the Premier, bent on having his say, "as I remarked, my son is unusually talented. Why, it is only necessary for him to read a book or manuscript once, just once, and he can reproduce it faultlessly character for character!"

"And, as I was saying when I was interrupted," retorted Old Su, "my daughter need never read anything more than once. She also has a remarkable talent for criticism. I have never known her to fail to judge literary values accurately. Furthermore, a manuscript reveals to her the personal virtues and shortcomings of the writer."

The Premier started in agitation. "Then, indeed, my friend," he said thoughtfully, "all the genius of the province of Szechwan is concentrated in your illustrious family."

At these words, Old Su recollected himself. Covering his confusion as best he could, he rose to take leave, pleading the lateness of the hour. The Premier produced a manuscript and handed it to Old Su, the old scholar. "May I beg you to give my son the benefit of your criticism on this essay?" he requested as he escorted his guest to the gate.

When his head had cleared from the fumes of the wine, Old Su repented bitterly of his boastful words.

"Alas, wretched tongue! Alas, drunken folly! Wang An-shih certainly means to ask the hand of Little Sister for his son, else why did he request me to criticize this manuscript? Very likely, too, he will begin negotiations at once. What excuse can I give without offending him? For, cost what it may, I will not give my daughter to such a conceited fop as the son must be." And the rest of the night he strove to find a way out of the difficulty.

When morning came, he had still found no solution. Sighing heavily he picked up the manuscript. To his surprise, it was logically conceived and exquisitely worded. "It is a masterpiece!" he exclaimed happily. "Every character a lustrous pearl, every line an embroidered thread of gold. But I shall let her decide."

Calling Little Sister's maid, he gave her the essay. "Take this to your young lady," he said. "It was given me to criticize, but I am busy now. Let your mistress do it for me."

The maid took the essay to Little Sister, who immediately became absorbed in it. Several times during the reading, she paused and sighed. When she had finished, she wrote on the cover: "Its merits — daring in expression, original in treatment; its faults — insincere in feeling, superficial in thought. Your showy qualities will gain you high honors, but, alas — will you reap them?"

When Old Su read Little Sister's criticism, he tore off

the entire cover and replaced it with a new one. Scarcely had he finished writing flattering compliments upon it, when a representative from the Premier was ushered in. The man received the manuscript from Old Su and furtively read the eulogy. Then, smiling with satisfaction, he spoke of everything under the sun except the real purpose of his visit. Old Su understood the visitor's assured smile, and he, too, chuckled slyly to himself.

"His Grace, the Premier, has a very remarkable son," finally ventured the representative, since Old Su failed to take the indirect hints which he threw out.

"Undoubtedly," replied Su, bowing and smiling benignly.

"And so different from most young men of his exalted station. He is brilliant and handsome, yet modest."

"Yes," politely agreed Su.

"Most young men are so proud and haughty that their eyes might well be set on the very top of their silly heads. Ah, me, sons such as that of the Premier and those of your honorable self are rare."

"My boys are nothing extraordinary," disclaimed Old Su politely.

"And Your Excellency is blessed, too, with a priceless daughter."

"Yes, I have a girl," guardedly admitted Su.

"How blessed is your illustrious house! Doubtless

many suitors have clamored for your honorable daughter's Horoscope of Eight Characters. Probably she is already betrothed?"

Old Su thought a moment. "If I say she is betrothed, then the stupid fellow will insist upon the name of her betrothed. If I tell him the truth, how can I help insulting Wang An-shih by an unequivocal refusal?" he agonized. "It would serve him right, though. What business did he have to send such a stupid and thick-skinned matchmaker?" Deciding, however, that truthtelling would be the lesser of the two evils, he finally said in a tone of great boredom, "No, she is not betrothed."

In spite of Old Su's efforts to ward off the proposal he so dreaded, the persistent matchmaker continued to throw out hints. The more Su tried to change the subject, the more resolutely his visitor clung to it. Finally, the matchmaker, unable to believe that Old Su would not jump at the proposed alliance, changed his tactics and stated in unmistakable terms the purpose of his visit.

"His Excellency's condescension," replied Old Su, "fills me with pleasure on one hand, regret on the other. The young man in question is undoubtedly a genius, and the house of Wang dates back seven times seven generations. Would that I could do as His Highness desires"—and here Old Su could not forbear to smile sardonically—"has not this proverb truthfully described his importance as

Premier—'above the myriad people: below one man only'?
Certainly his subjects should gratify his every wish. But,
even at the risk of his displeasure, I would rather not burden his son with so unprepossessing a bride as my daughter. She is unworthy of the honor of having so handsome
a husband. Be so kind, therefore, as to convey my appreciation and regret to His Excellency," and, bowing, he dis-
missed the unwelcome guest.

Bewildered by this curt and unexpected refusal, and
afraid to return to Wang An-shih without some plausible
excuse, the thwarted matchmaker decided to learn all he
could about Little Sister. In this, he was more successful
than he had been in the other business.

Although her brothers were many years her senior, Little Sister did not stand in awe of them. From childhood
she had looked upon them as obliging playmates. Big Su
used often to write nonsense rhymes to tease her about her
rather homely appearance, and she would retaliate in kind.
The Su family had many friends, and in time these
rhymes became well known around the town.

The matchmaker memorized as many of these rhymes
as he could. Then he went back to the yamen and reported
the result of his visit. As he expected, Wang An-shih felt
greatly insulted at Old Su's outspoken refusal, and angry
at his own loss of face. And, as the matchmaker had also
expected, the Premier began by abusing him.

"Your Excellency, with all respect to Miss Su, she is not worthy to be Your Excellency's daughter-in-law," the matchmaker hastened to say; "for in truth her ugly and repulsive face makes her the laughingstock of everyone. Her forehead protrudes like an overhanging cliff, and her eyes are so deeply embedded in her face that they look like muddy ruts. I should not wonder but that she may be a hunchback," he added for good measure. "Besides, as Your Excellency knows, the father and brothers have unpleasant faces as well," and he went on to repeat the nonsense rhymes written in fun. Thus he succeeded in appeasing the wrath of the Premier, who consoled himself with the belief that Old Su had exaggerated Little Sister's accomplishments, and that he would not have her for a daughter-in-law now even if Old Su were willing. "For," he argued, "all the brilliancy in the world cannot discount a clown's face."

Meanwhile, Little Sister did not lack suitors. In each case Old Su requested the prospective husband to submit an essay, which he then passed on to his daughter. But Little Sister found flaws in each and every manuscript submitted. Old Su became more and more perplexed. One day, however, he found this criticism on the cover of an essay.

Today, an earnest Hsiu-Ts'ai,
Tomorrow, a brilliant scholar;

Too bad the Su Brothers live in your generation,
Otherwise, you alone would deserve admiration.

In spite of this half-mocking verse, Su saw that his
daughter was really impressed by the writer's ability and
personality. At once he gave orders that, when the scholar
Chin Shao-yu called, he should be admitted. Time passed,
and Shao-yu did not appear. Mystified, Old Su made
secret attempts to identify the young man. Shao-yu himself heard of all this in time, but still he did not present
himself.

"For all I know," thought the young man, "Little Sister's wit and learning may be exaggerated. Besides, I hear
she is homely. Now, accomplishments and intellect are
all very well in a girl and quite worthy of admiration, but
suppose she is actually so ugly that I feel repulsion at the
sight of her? And is she really such a wonderful scholar?
Beauty fades with time, and I love not beauty for beauty's
sake, but a wife ought to have at least passable good looks.
What if I married her and then discovered her wit to be
shallow, her pride intolerable, her looks unbearable? Why
should I not watch her unobserved and test her in conver-
sation before I present myself?"

An opportunity soon came for him to do this. He
learned that on the first day of the Second Moon Miss
Su had planned to offer sacrifices at a certain temple. Shao-

yu dressed himself in the robes of a Taoist priest with chains of prayer beads around his neck and placed himself at the temple gate, holding a mendicant's bowl in his hands. Before long, Little Sister appeared, riding in a palanquin. He followed her into the Sacrificial Hall. To his great joy, although her face was not of the goose-egg shape most often lauded by poets and connoisseurs of feminine beauty, it looked very pleasing and most intelligent.

"Not bad," he said to himself; "in fact, I prefer it to the regular contours of the egg oval. And how gracefully she carries herself ! Her gestures suggest willow leaves in the breeze, and her movements bespeak delicacy and precision. Now to test her wit."

When the sacrifices had burned to ashes he followed her out into the courtyard. Making a deep obeisance, he held out his bowl toward her. "May the young lady have happiness and long life in doing good works," he murmured.

"You, oh Taoist, what virtue and merit have you who dare to hope for alms?" she asked.

"May the young lady be a life-giving plant, free from the hundred human ills," he chanted.

"I would not give one cash for verbal flowers such as these," she retorted.

"Good little woman, well said," he mocked.

"Crazy Taoist, it is hard to acquire merit because of such as you!" she exclaimed as she stepped into her waiting palanquin.

An old retainer, hearing the Taoist's impertinence to his mistress, was about to rebuke him when he heard a voice calling to Shao-yu, "O Master, come hither to change your robes." His curiosity aroused, the old servant followed the voice and perceived a young valet with a pile of neatly folded clothes in his arms. "Who is he whom you called master?" asked the retainer.

"That is my master, Chin Shao-yu, the most brilliant and talented Hsiu Ts'ai in the world, on the word of no less an exalted person than your old master. And the very man your master has been searching for," boasted the valet.

Upon returning home, the old servant lost no time in relating the incident of the morning. Little Sister heard of it through her maid, while she was having her long tresses oiled and combed that evening. Through the recital she smiled mischievously but remained silent.

The very next day, Shao-yu appeared before Old Su and requested Little Sister's Horoscope of Eight Characters. Old Su joyfully consented, and upon being pressed to set the auspicious date for the wedding he consulted his daughter.

"Tell him," replied Little Sister, "that he must first

pass the examination for the Degree of the Raised Man.
This is the Second Moon; on the third day of the Third
Moon the examination will commence. Until then, let
him prepare himself."

In the middle of the Third Moon Shao-yu, having won
the coveted degree with honors, returned to beg Old Su
to set the wedding day. Little Sister consented demurely
to her father's wishes and the wedding took place. After
the ceremony, when the guests had feasted until mid-
night, Shao-yu traced his steps to the nuptial chamber.
He tried the door and found it securely latched on the
inside. Looking around the antechamber, he noticed a
table on which were placed writing brushes, paper, ink,
three wine pots and three wine cups. A young maid stood
near the table.

"Tell your mistress," directed Shao-yu, "that the
bridegroom is here. Why not open the door?"

"My mistress," replied the maid, making a deep bow,
"ordered me to stay here to await the bridegroom. On the
table are writing materials, and here are three sealed envelopes. When the bridegroom shall have successfully
passed the three tests in them, then, and only then, will
the door of the Perfumed Chamber be opened to him."

Shao-yu took the three envelopes from her outstretched
hand. "And what is the meaning of these?" he inquired
in amazement, pointing to the three wine pots and cups.

"Inside this pot of green jade is fragrant wine," she explained. "If the bridegroom is successful in all three tests, he may drink three cups of fragrant wine out of the jade cup, and will have immediate access to the Perfumed Chamber. Inside this pot of bright silver is amber tea. If the bridegroom is successful in two of the three tests, he may drink two cups of amber tea out of the silver cup and then may try again tomorrow. Inside this pot of white porcelain is clean water. If the bridegroom is successful in only one out of the three tests, then he may drink one cup of clear water to quench his thirst and must remain in solitude in the antechamber for three months to sharpen his wits."

"He, ho," thought the bridegroom, "so Little Sister is as doubtful of the keenness of my wits as I was of hers. Well, she may give me three hundred tests and not find me wanting."

Opening the first envelope, he took out a piece of shining white silk, delicate as gossamer. On it was written a poem of four lines.

"You are to write a companion poem to it," directed the maid. "The theme of each of your lines must be sought in the hidden significance of each of the four corresponding lines in my mistress' poem."

Shao-yu, his brush poised in mid-air, chuckled. "The little tease! So she recognized the Crazy Taoist! I see, I see. The key to her poem must signify 'Heaven Fated Begging Taoist.' " Setting to work, he soon finished his poem, which the maid thrust under the door.

Little Sister in the Perfumed Chamber smiled.

Opening the second envelope, he found another four lines of poetry. "Each of these lines refers to an ancient hero," explained the maid. Shao-yu thought a few moments, and wrote the correct names, which the maid again thrust through the crevice.

Little Sister in the Perfumed Chamber nodded with delight.

"Now for the third," laughed Shao-yu. In the third envelope he found only seven characters. "You yourself are to write seven characters which together with those in the envelope will form a perfect antithetical couplet," directed the maid, who herself was no mean scholar.

"Easy!" he cried as he read the line. He set to work, but, try as he would, he could not find seven characters which would match the seven which he had found in the third envelope and still conform to the rules of versification. Unable to think sitting down, he began to pace back and forth. Finding no inspiration, he stepped out on the balcony and gazed pleadingly at the silvery moon. Roguishly the stars twinkled. He scratched his head, he caressed his mustache, grown in honor of the marriage. He chanted poem after poem from the famous T'ang

poets. Still no inspiration. He sighed, he groaned, he
fidgeted. And all in vain. Finally, with beads of perspira-
tion on his forehead, face uplifted heavenward, one hand
motioning as if to close a door, the other as if to shut out
the moon from his sight, he murmured over and over the
seven characters: "Closing door, shut out moon from
windows."

Little Sister in the Perfumed Chamber giggled.

Now Big Su, having drunk a great deal of wine at the
marriage feast, could not sleep. Stepping out on the balcony to cool his head, he heard Shao-yu murmuring the
first line of the couplet and saw him gesticulating.

"So, Little Sister, is this the way you treat your bridegroom!" he chuckled silently, taking in the situation.
Leaning forward, he started to call to the hapless Shao-yu,
when he noticed the bride peeping from behind a half-
opened window of the Perfumed Chamber. The more
violent the bridegroom's gestures, the more merrily she
laughed. Finally, unable to control her silent mirth, she
covered her face with both hands. Big Su picked up a
handful of pebbles from a near-by jardiniere and threw
them into the lily pond in the garden just beneath the
balcony. Drops of water splashed into Shao-yu's face.
He came to himself with a start and looked downward.
The surface of the water, disturbed by the stones, rippled
into widening circles. The moonlight danced quiveringly

over it as it reflected the sky above. With a shout of joy, he rushed back into the antechamber, seized a brush and finished the couplet:

> Closing door, shut out moon from windows.
> Throwing stone, open up sky in waters.

Big Su waited until the door of the Perfumed Chamber had been unlatched and closed again behind Shao-yu. Then he yawned sleepily and returned to his room.

Section VII

CHINA IN WARTIME

I.

WOMEN OF CHINA—DEFEND
YOUR COUNTRY!

"We must give up everything, even our lives, to support our fighters at the front."

THE nation is facing the gravest crisis in its history. War is a terrible thing. It means that we must sacrifice a large number of our soldiers; masses of our innocent people; much of the nation's wealth and resources, and see ruthlessly destroyed a construction that we have been working upon so successfully for ten years. But sometimes it is necessary that we make the supreme sacrifice for the sake of our national honor. Now that our government clearly has demonstrated that we have borne all suffering that a self-respecting people can possibly bear, we must unhesitatingly and with courage throw the last ounce of strength and energy into an effort to secure national survival. There is nothing left for us to do but to obey the orders of the government and fortify others to do likewise.

Every one of us Chinese must fight according to our ability, in order to preserve national unity and defend ourselves against aggression. We women are citizens just as much as are our men. Our positions, our capabilities, and our lines of usefulness may be different, but each must do that which best can be done to contribute our share to rescue our nation from defeat and slavery.

Wherever there is work for our hands to do, we must strive to do it. In Spain women stood in the fighting lines with their men; and during the World War in every country they gave of their best to aid in the realization of victory. We Chinese women are not one whit less patriotic or less courageous or less capable of physical endurance than our sisters of other lands, and that we shall show the world.

While during wartime the men are the fighters, it is the women who bear the brunt of carrying on at the rear. We must encourage the men and let them know that we are in our own way holding on and not letting them down; that we are just as ready to give up everything, even our lives, to support our fighters.

The fighting morale of our men at the front depends on how much support the rear can give. We must never forget that. And we must remember always that a final national victory, no matter how belated it may be in coming, will erase forever the "humiliation days" that have for so long crowded our calendar and will remove the sorrow that for years past has bent our heads and bowed our hearts.

2.

DUTY OF CHINESE WOMEN
IN THE WAR

"Women must assist in upholding the morale of the nation in its gravest trial."

WOMEN must stay behind the lines in time of war and carry on men's work so that the latter can go to the front and defend the country. If they are determined to fight in the front line there will be room. But we have not been trained or prepared for that kind of work. Personally I doubt if the physical strength and endurance of women could equal that of men destined to face the enemy; so they must help behind the lines.

We have to teach them not to be afraid of anything and to make the great sacrifices that must be made by a country so ruthlessly invaded as is China. The cruelty of the cold-blooded murder that is being inflicted on the population of China by the Japanese must be made understandable to the people.

But if citizens are to be killed, we want those who can

to make the sacrifice of their lives helping the men at the front in any way possible. The women have to assist in upholding the morale of the nation in its gravest trial; in obeying implicitly the orders of the government, and having those orders carried out by all citizens; in suppressing rumors, and, by economies, conserving the nation's foodstuffs and apparel. The time will probably come, too, when the agricultural work in the fields, and many of the ordinary occupations of men, will have to be done by the women, so they must organize and get ready for it. I think that the greatest contribution we can make is our strength and determination to make any and all sacrifices for the preservation of the nation.

Women are gradually coming into prominence the world around, in spheres that used not so long ago to be considered as preserves essentially belonging to men. A similar phenomenon is happening in China, and in this country women are finding their way into many avenues of endeavor where men used to hold monopolistic sway. But, fortunately or unfortunately, we cannot do without the men, nor can they do without us.

When the transpacific telephone was inaugurated, I seized the opportunity to voice a thought on the subject of how women might be able to assist in the ending of such calamities as are now devastating parts of China, and will in the course of time spread ruin over large areas. Then

I asked Mrs. Roosevelt, the wife of the President of the United States, if the women of the world could not be got together under her aegis to do something to prevent wars.

It was merely a voice calling over the waste of waters, for it was obvious that Japan was preparing rapidly to descend upon China with a repetition of the savage bloodthirstiness that had characterized her in 1932 when she ordered her airplanes to fly out of the dawn and rain bombs on the innocent, sleeping population of Chapei.

3.

ARE TREATIES DEAD?

"The civilized nations have permitted this collapse of treaties and twentieth century revival of brutal civilian murder."

My mind still holds painful recollections of tragic accidents in and near Shanghai[1] which caused death to some, injury to others, and suffering to many American and other residents. Both the Generalissimo and I deeply deplore these accidents, and grieve with those who have been bereaved or who have suffered, especially as among those killed and injured were personal friends of ours. Our government in so far as possible is doing its best to prevent a recurrence of such accidents, which could never have happened, however, had it not been for the fact that the Japanese brought war into Shanghai by using the International Settlement as a base for military operations. And they brought the war to China to destroy her before she could complete the reorganization work which has been going on in recent years with such great promise and success.

[1] Written in 1937.

Out of a united China was emerging an orderly state. The Japanese did not want that and are, therefore, striking in many places to destroy it. That they have utter disregard for the security of the lives and property of both foreigners and Chinese has been seen in Shanghai.

Any American living in China knows that whenever Japanese establish themselves in China, they systematically set up bases for the destruction of our people. They have done so by military action, by the demoralizing effects of opium and narcotics, or by the instigation of plots to undermine the authority of our Central Government.

The Japanese militarists lie to their people and they lie to the world. They seize upon any excuse to justify any evil thing they plan to do. For example, they are now publishing the gross calumny that we Chinese are spreading cholera germs among their troops in Shanghai and that they intend to take reprisals. What reprisals? gas? and why? Is it because for weeks now they have not been able to bring China to her knees as they boasted? They have used the concentrated weight of the most modern implements of war—navy, artillery, air force, tanks and army,—but our soldiers are still holding them.

You can see by what Japan is now doing in China that she is sinister, ruthless, well armed, well organized, and acting on a preconceived plan. For years she has been preparing for this very attempt to conquer China even if she has to annihilate the Chinese to do so. Curiously, no other nation seems to care to stop it. Is it because the flood of calculated falsehoods that Japan broadcasts daily is believed? Or is it that she has been able to hypnotize the statesmen of the world? She seems to have secured their spellbound silence by uttering the simple magical formula: "This is not a war, but merely an incident." Even the declaration by the Japanese Premier, Prince Konoye, that Japan intends to "beat China to her knees, so that she may no longer have the spirit to fight," does not seem to have had any effect in awakening the world to a realization of the catastrophe which is now developing.

It was to avert such a catastrophe that the great powers signed the Nine-Power Treaty, which was specially created to safeguard China from invasion by Japan. They signed the Kellogg Peace Pact to prevent war, and they organized the League of Nations to make it doubly certain that aggressive nations would be quickly prevented from inflicting unjustified harm upon their weaker fellows. But, strange to say, all these treaties appear to have crumbled to dust in a way that has not hitherto been equaled in history. Worse than that, all complex structure under International Law which was gradually built up to regulate the conduct of war and protect noncombatants seems to have crashed with the treaties. So we have a reversion to the day of the savages when the stronger tried to exterminate the weaker, to kill not only their warriors but their very families, their women and their children. That is what Japan is trying to do in China. But it is the civilized nations who have really permitted this collapse of treaties and this twentieth century revival of the wholesale brutal murder of innocent civilians. They allowed it to begin in China, in 1931, when Japan seized Manchuria. They permitted it to be continued in 1932 at Shanghai when Japan bombed the sleeping population in Chapei, and they now acquiesce in its resumption all over China on a gigantic scale.

The consequence of this is that the Japanese feel free to destroy schools and cultural institutions wherever they can. Nankai University and the Women's Normal School and the Engineering College at Tientsin have been wiped out completely. What was not demolished by bombs was later destroyed by Japanese with kerosene. They attacked the University of Shanghai, known as the Shanghai Baptist College, demolished the Tung-Chi University at Woosung, bombed the Central University at Nanking and the Baldwin Girls' School at Nanchang. Added to this, they deliberately bombed and destroyed the American Mission Hospital at Tungchow, the Chinese Red Cross Hospital at Chenju and various Red Cross ambulances. They also shot from the air the British Ambassador and tried to bomb him as well, but with brazen effrontery their Foreign Minister now says that no Japanese planes would do such a thing. Fortunately the British Military Attaché identified the planes and is able to disprove the lie that is now being told by the Japanese Government.

If such calculated destruction of life and property can be accomplished before the so-called hostilities have developed, what is going to happen now that the Japanese have begun to carry out their threat to crush China completely? Whatever will be the end, a beginning has been made to demolish everything Chinese, as well as to destroy with savage blows those valuable American religious and cultural enterprises that have been erected in China in the course of years. Even American institutions (contributed to so liberally by the people of America) which have done so much for the progress of China are destined to be severely crippled in their work, if not destroyed, should the Japanese have their way, since the Japanese condemn them as being the fostering places of future resistance. Indeed, so intense is their hate that they are bent upon wrecking or eradicating all foreign influences, cultural as well as commercial, and the sooner that fact is understood abroad the better.

In all this I greatly fear for the safety of American and European women and children. We Chinese valued highly the services that missionaries of all countries have given our people, and it is with sincere regret that I find myself compelled to assist in arranging for their evacuation within the immediate future. People in America and Europe may rest assured that the National Government of China will do everything in its power to see that those who are escaping the menace of war are transported to the coast, though naturally some will wish to stay and suffer with us. We want to defend them, but we may not even be able to defend ourselves. Japan blockades our coast and demands that the nations stop supplying us with arms and munitions, while she may be supplied with all the instruments of murder that she desires.

Surely such a monstrous demand has never been put to the world before, and we hope it will not be entertained. But to make it, Japan must be singularly confident of her influence and power over the world, especially as, in addition to getting international assistance to tie our hands, she now declares her intention to bring China to her knees as if she were sure no one would say her nay. It may be no one will, but if the nations become accessories to this mass murder and criminal destruction, then civilization has surely reached its end.

Yet China, so often accused of cowardice, unprepared as she is, has decided no longer to suffer the aggressions, the brutalities, and the insults of so gross a tyrant, and is fighting for her very existence.

In this fight the loyal support of our compatriots abroad

will be a great factor in our final victory. I wish to thank
our overseas Chinese for their generous contributions to
the war chest and to assure them that we in China are
striving to prove worthy of their unfailing co-operation
and encouragement in the defense of the land of our ancestors. I also wish to thank the many foreign friends of China
who, by their expressions of sympathy and moral support,
have heartened us in our tasks. Foreign sympathy is necessary, for we depend upon the wisdom and the justice of the
nations to save the world from the consequences of the
calculated falsehoods daily emanating from Japan, and
hope that our cause and our efforts will secure support of
the treaties which China has so faithfully adhered to and
upheld.

The militarists of Japan have already shown the world
their contempt for any codes of international honor. In
addition they have dragged the mantle of their own Samu-
rai in the mud and have cast their own famed Bushido
(their boasted creed of chivalrous conduct) into the gutter,
and they do not seem ashamed that the people of the
world should witness such betrayal. The reason, no doubt,
is that they are convinced that the powers dare not oppose
them. So they are proceeding with plans of conquest confident that they will be able to devastate China and, in
time, drive out Western cultural and commercial influences, so that, if we Chinese cannot prevent them, they

may erect upon the ashes of China a world-shaking Japanese continental empire. It will not be founded upon international ethics (for Japan has already crippled those), but upon militarized force. At least they expect to control all lands where the Oriental races live, and eventually determine international conduct and policies.

With that extravagant aim in view, is it any wonder that Japan asks how China dares to have the spirit to fight? Well might the princely Premier of Japan ask the question! Hitherto it has been China who has trembled while the rest of the world has wondered why she would not fight. Now we have the ironic picture of China fighting, not only for her sovereign rights and existence, but also for the sanctity of treaties, while the foreign nations watch their rights and interests being destroyed and their people put to flight. To see the great powers accepting such a situation must be regarded by Japanese militarists as a delightfully encouraging spectacle, for they can think they have at last been able, with no difficulty, to sweep Occidental prestige clean from the boards of the Orient.

And we wonder, does this indicate the fall of civilization? Look at the mass murders of Chinese in various places by bombs, by the naval guns mounted on miles of men-of-war anchored in the sheltered harbor of Shanghai, by machine guns and by rifles. Look at the homes and businesses that have been swept up in savage flames or been blasted into dust. Look at the square miles of blood-stained debris heaped with dead. Look at the fleeing thousands of Chinese and foreigners, screaming, panic-stricken, running for their lives — indeed, hundreds of thousands of Chinese mothers and children, homeless, foodless, bereft of everything, leaving their homes shattered and burning behind them when they tried to flee from the horrors of Shanghai. Look what terrible tragedy overtook them. Thousands of them were crowded in the South Station to get into a train when Japanese bombers came overhead, dropped bombs upon them and blew three hundred of them to ghastly fragments, while over four hundred were wounded. No soldier was anywhere near the station, so there was no justification for the terrible massacre. The editor of the *North China Daily News,* the leading British paper in the Far East, described the barbarous act "as wanton a crime against humanity as can well be conceived." Only a few days later when hundreds of refugees who had managed to escape Shanghai were sitting in their train at Sungkiang Station, some miles out, they were similarly attacked, and another three hundred were blown into eternity by being reduced to torn fragments of flesh while hundreds more were seriously wounded. Not a soldier was on the train.

The chief American paper in the Far East, the *Shang-*

hai Evening Post and Mercury, editorially cried "murder" at the first outrage, and, when the second happened, declared that there were no words in the dictionary to describe such monstrous deeds. At the market town of Changshu, not far from Shanghai, where there were no soldiers at all, Japanese bombers flew down one side of the crowded main street, machine-gunned the people and bombed the houses and shops. Then the planes flew up the other side repeating the deadly operation until hundreds of people were corpses and the whole street a mass of demolished buildings and debris. This type of massacre is going on throughout the country and is bound to be intensified once the army air force has prepared its fields.

Tell me, is the silence of Western nations in the face of such massacres, such demolition of homes and dislocation of businesses, a sign of the triumph of civilization with its humanitarianism, its codes of conduct, its chivalry, and its claims of Christian influence? Or is the spectacle of the first-class powers, all standing silently in a row as if so stupefied by Japan that they do not utter a reproach, the forerunner of the collapse of international ethics, of Christian guidance and conduct, and the death knell of the supposed moral superiority of the Occidental?

If the whole of the Occidental world is indifferent to all this, and abandons its treaties, we in China, who have labored for years under the stigma of cowards, will do our best. We will try to fight till we win or till we are really beaten to our broken knees, even if our good earth, with all its history and cares, is steeped with blood, swept by fire, and destroyed.

4.

DURING AN AIR RAID

*"I see the Japanese bombers coming . . . we
are defendants in an undeclared war — a
violent unwarranted, unjustified aggression."*

I AM writing this while I sit waiting for the Japanese air
raiders to come. The alarm sounded fifteen minutes ago.
I came outside as I always do, to watch the raid and more
particularly to observe how our defense is conducted. When
the planes arrive, I will write down in order what I see.

During all this time since Japan started pounding us
at Shanghai the sufferings of our people have been indescribable. Foreign military experts declare that nowhere
in the world, even in Spain or during the World War,
have they seen such pitiless, calculated air bombardment
and artillery fire as is being directed by the Japanese on our
ill-equipped but gallant soldiers. These experts say that
they cannot understand how human flesh can stand what
our troops have stood and are standing.

In the World War the air bases were hundreds of miles
from the front. Bombers could manage perhaps two trips
a day, if not intercepted by a strong force of defense planes.
But at Shanghai we now have no planes to oppose the Jap-

anese, and they have to travel only, at the most, five miles back to their base to reload. They just cruise over our lines, dropping their loads en masse, having nothing to do but keep out of range of what little anti-aircraft fire we can put up. Perhaps you wonder why we have no air force to oppose the 400-odd planes which the Japanese have based at Shanghai alone (altogether they have over 3,000). You must remember that China's air force is less than five years old, and several of those years were wasted through lack of experience in handling the new type of weapon.

This caused us to be without adequate air defenses when the invasion came and compelled us to place large orders in America and elsewhere and hope to have them filled as quickly as possible. We knew what to expect from Japan but we never, in our most pessimistic moods, imagined that America. . . .

Now I see the Japanese bombers coming — "three — six — nine," cries little Jimmie, who is taken with me because he has eyes like gimlets.

It is now 2:42 P.M. It is a bright afternoon. Above there are cumulus clouds. High above them, orderly mackerel. Three heavy Japanese bombers come through a blue cleft between the piles of cumulus, heading from the north due south. Three more follow. Anti-aircraft guns put clusters of black smoke puffs around the first three. Now they are bobbing up about the second three. Here come three more — so there are nine altogether. High above the clouds I hear pursuit planes. The detonations of anti-aircraft guns are away in front of me, near the military airfield, which the bombers are heading for. Some of our pursuit planes appear. They have flown behind clouds. The sound of machine-gun fire is now high above me. Above the clouds the pilots are fighting. The nine bombers proceed in steady progress across the city. They have to keep their line if they wish to hit their objectives. The first three are now over the south city wall.

2:46 P.M. Great spouts of flame; columns of smoke and dust ascend. They have dropped several bombs. Then they scatter. Some of our pursuit planes are attacking. North of me a vicious dogfight is going on. It started at 2:34 P.M. All the bombers now are out of sight, in the clouds, but some Japanese pursuits are still being harassed by our fighters.

2:50 P.M. There is a dogfight in the northwest. An enemy plane, with a Hawk pursuit close on his tail, dives fast. He is out of sight behind Purple Mountain. The combatants are sweeping in and out of the clouds.[2] The

[2] A Japanese plane was noticed doing a number of great vertical circles until it disappeared behind Purple Mountain. Next day the plane was found crashed on a hillside. The pilot had been hit by seventeen bullets. He apparently fell dead in such a position in his seat that his plane kept up its speed in large loops until it struck the hill.

first three bombers, having dropped their loads, are fast disappearing in the east, bound back to their base near Shanghai. The other six, scattered by the pursuits, are circling in and out of the clouds to the south trying to get a bearing on their objectives.

2:51 P.M. Suddenly to the southwest of the city smoke and flame and dust in great columns appear. Some more bombers have completed their mission.

2:55 P.M. While dogfights are still making the northern heavens rattle with machine-gun fire, other bombers sweep to the south and drop their bombs on the airdrome.

2:56 P.M. More explosives are deposited in the same locality. High in the air, a little to the west, there is a dogfight. Another is going on over the city, in full view of all who can see. A Chinese Hawk is chasing a Japanese monoplane. They are looping and turning and diving—and zooming up again. Their machine guns are clattering. The raider seems to have our man; no, he has escaped. They sweep away in wide circles and fly fast at each other again. There is heavy anti-aircraft fire at the bombers now escaping. The Japanese plane seems to stall in mid-air. He is hit. The Hawk sweeps round to attack again. The Japanese pauses awhile, then goes into a headlong dive; flames stream out; the doomed machine is heading for a thickly populated part of the city near the south gate. Orange flame, with a long comet tail of smoke, cleaves through the sky. The Hawk flies in circles, watching his enemy crash.

2:58 P.M. Now the raider hits the top of the city, as it were. There is a great burst of black smoke and flame. Then comes yellow smoke — a house is burning. The Hawk still circles, then flies northward where other dog-fights are making noises in the sky. In and out of the clouds to the northeast and northwest planes are fighting.

3:10 P.M. One of our planes dives fast, with a great roar. From behind the clouds come three Japanese planes, all attacking him. He has disappeared from view, on his tail a Japanese plunging like a plummet.

3:17 P.M. There are no planes now in sight. Engines in the distance are just audible. Only a column of smoke, from where the Japanese plane crashed to death in the city, is visible.

3:20 P.M. There is now no sound in the skies. The raid lasted about forty minutes. So I shall go, as usual, and inspect the damage, to find out the score of gains and losses. I drive to where the plane crashed. People are in the streets as if nothing unusual had occurred. Mothers and children who saw or heard a flaming monster roar through the air near them and crash into a house near by, with a mighty burst of flame, appear as if nothing of moment concerned them. Firemen are at the scene with hose and buckets. The fire is out. Getting through doors to a mass of smoking, charred timber, I am told the remains of the plane are there. It is difficult to find them. I am also told that the badly disfigured head of a Japanese is visible among the charred mass, but I do not look. I am anxious to discover if any of my countrymen have suffered. No one knows. A policeman tells me they will have to remove the debris before they can find out.

On reaching home, I learn that three Japanese planes have been shot down, and two more earlier in the morning. These two were intercepted and did not reach Nanking. Altogether, nine two-engined heavy bombers (carrying crews of six each) and six pursuits raided the city. Our losses were two forced landings — but four injured pilots, one dead.

When I was interrupted by the raid, I was writing that we never, in our most pessimistic moods, imagined that America would place an embargo on shipments of equipment and prevent American instructors coming to China by refusing them passports. For we are defendants in an undeclared war — a violent, unwarranted, unjustified aggression. Our very life is being strangled from us — there is a blockade of our coast; our railways are being bombed along their whole lengths; and worse than all are the monstrous massacres of our defenseless people that the Japanese are regularly carrying out with their bombing planes. Homes are demolished; scores, hundreds of people are mangled at a time, and hundreds more are wounded. Destruction of railways, machine-gunning of highways and junks, and the consequent stagnation of business are bringing ruin to those who persist in defying the bombings.

Yet, though all this horror threatens the very basis of civilization, and though the violent contempt of treaties and codes of international law menaces the foundation of human security, we find America operating to prevent our securing the means of self-defense, and, therefore, aiding our enemy to fulfill her threat that she will beat us to our knees. Is it any wonder that the sight of the champion of justice thus succoring the aggressor and actually encouraging him in his inhuman acts staggered us?

Not only were we amazed at America's attitude, but we could do nothing else but feel that we who had loyally adhered to treaties and to the principles laid down in the Covenant of the League of Nations and who had suffered for it by the loss of Manchuria were simply being struck in the face by the great republic whom we had been taught to look up to with respect and, indeed, to emulate. When we saw America yield to the preposterous demands of Japan to respect her blockade by unshipping American airplanes (for which we had paid cash) from American ships at San Diego, can you blame us for thinking that the end had come to all professions of faith in those princi-

ples that are deemed to be good and honest and just?
That act, in the face of an undeclared war, of an outrageous blockade, of a world-wide declaration that China
was to be crushed to her knees, of the infliction of the
worst kind of inhuman cruelty on our people over great
areas of our country, hurt us sorely.

Fortunately, the contumely which the Japanese heaped
on Occidental efforts to see justice done to China, plus
the continued inhumanities of the Japanese in various
directions, brought the officials of America to a stage
where they could no longer shut their eyes to what was
going on, and the President delivered a really masterful
exposition of America's views. It was belated but nevertheless welcome, as evidence of justification for our faith
that America could not be a party to the calculated ex-
termination of the Chinese as a nation.

The subsequent statement from the American Depart-
ment of State drove the nails a bit deeper, we hope, into
the coffin of Japan; and we were correspondingly encouraged in our belief that some effort would be made to give
deep consideration to our cause, with the object of having
treaties respected and so effecting the withdrawal of the
enemy from our soil before it should be too late. The enemy accepted the new attitude of America with ostensible
disdain, but there must be misgivings in high circles in
Japan.

If the people of Japan knew what was going on in China, I feel sure that the militarists would not be able to continue with their warfare — to say nothing of their ruthlessness. They are deliberately destroying Japan's greatest market and they are not letting the people of Japan know anything about it. All radios are censored, as well as all newspapers. All that the people are told is that China has insulted their country, has defied her, and has threatened the lives of Japanese people in China.

At the outset the militarists promised their country, however, that their proceedings would be concluded in China in a week or two and that Japan would be able to reap rich harvests from the militarists' program. How they are going to explain what is happening it is difficult to see. About their failures at Shanghai they say little, but they print colorful pictures of the might of their arms against the provincial troops in the north, where their mechanized units have full play. From Japan herself, however, there is no hope of justice until the militarists have been put in their place.

5.

NO FRUITS FOR THE AGGRESSOR!

"We are fighting and dying in defense of our soil, and for the principles that other nations profess to espouse; we only ask that these nations demonstrate that there can be no fruits for the aggressor from this barbarous invasion."

IF THE millions of women of China, who are already victims of the horrors of undeclared warfare, could make their voice heard through their grief, their tears, and the smoke of their burnt homes, it is certain that American womanhood would be shocked into acute realization of the far-reaching consequences of the calamities now threatening civilization. There would be little tolerance for the attempt to justify the commission of unparalleled plunder, rape, and massacre in this twentieth century on the ground that such things have been done before. Instead, there is every reason to believe that the women of America would respond to the alarm which the women of China could raise, and would be inflexible in their demands that durable barricades against the disintegration of civilization be set up before it is too late.

If ever there was menace in the throbbing of distant drums, it is now. Nor is there even the shadow of protection to be had by the shutting of eyes to the possibilities of world war, by sheltering behind the slender stockades of visionary speculation or by hiding behind the wagon wheels of pacific theories. The bow and the arrow and the bowie knife have been replaced by far-reaching high explosives and exquisite instruments of destruction. But the holocaust in China, lighted as it has been by torn treaties and agreements, proves, surely and bitterly, that the forked tongue and the cloven hoof are still with us, and have to be reckoned with just as much as ever. So it is proved that reliance can no longer be placed upon mere signed undertakings, be they dignified treaties or simple letters.

Stark realism is necessary now more than at any time in modern history. If the women of America will be realistic in viewing and estimating the happenings in China, they can do infinite good in assisting to break down misguided conceptions, and set up, as they used to help set up in old frontier days, collective action for mutual defense against a common enemy.

Only by collective action — economic, if no other — will it be possible to arrest the collapse of democratic ideas of liberty and justice, and prevent America, and particularly smaller, weaker, and less fortunate democratic countries from being laid open to what Mr. Cordell Hull described as "unpredictable hazards," but which are really definitely predictable if eyes are not deliberately closed to the infamies now being perpetrated in China.

We people of China appreciate the great and growing sympathy of the American people. We know full well that governmental action on our behalf is difficult, owing to a variety of circumstances, and we do not expect America, or any other country, to fight our battles for us. But we are unable to understand why the civilized nations are content to permit without protest the gross inhumanities and monstrous organized robberies which are being perpetrated all over China as a definite part of a deliberate attempt to destroy the Chinese race and effect the conquest of our ancient country.

After all, respect for the territorial and administrative integrity of our country was solemnly agreed upon by a congress of nations. If that agreement was not to be upheld in case of violation, what good was served in having the treaty in the first place? What good is any treaty, may we, who are being despoiled, tortured, and done to death, ask if no retribution is to be exacted from nations who scorn it when suitable to them; and worse, who deluge a country in blood and raze it by fire in order to conquer it? Nor, with all deference, can we understand why any country should affirm that it "should uphold the principles of the sanctity of treaties and of faithful observance of international agreements" if the upholding of such principles is contentedly defined as mere reiteration of the principles or failure to violate them.

It seems to our simple minds, if I may be pardoned for saying so, that if a nation is a signatory to those principles, then surely that nation is both morally and legally obligated to act with other signatories in restraining, by some means or other, not necessarily force, any nation that dares to violate those principles. Or, again, it is puzzling to the Chinese mind why anyone should bother subscribing to something that seems to mean a lot, but in reality, when the test comes, resolves itself into meaning nothing. Here, in point of fact, is the loophole offering escape without penalty to any unscrupulous nation desiring to free itself from observance of any treaties which become irksome or which may obstruct some design of an aggressor upon the territory of a neighbor.

It is said, and it is true, that all nations should strive to be friendly. But should such friendship be maintained at the expense of a great and ancient country like China by submitting to or apparently acquiescing in aggression by Japan ?

We, in China, are thankful that the policy of America has been clarified in general terms. Something specific, however, must be done immediately to compel Japan to understand that her violation of treaties, and her revolting inhumanities and destruction in China, can neither be condoned nor be excused. Above all, Japan must be given unequivocally to understand that no so-called peace will be connived at or be tolerated which will in any way sacrifice, or infringe upon, the sovereignty or territorial integrity of China. China has loyally adhered to those fundamental principles which underlie international order and without which there can be nothing but international anarchy.

To the womanhood of America I can only appeal for careful understanding of the ferociously relentless progress of the aggression. I can only urge them to weigh its aims, and the consequences to the rest of the world if those aims are achieved. I ask them to think of the terrible carnage and suffering; of the destruction of means of livelihood; of the ghastly efforts that the Japanese are making to annihilate our culture, our civilization, and our people. We have never ceased to resist; we will not cease. Our spirit is undaunted, even though our means are jeopardized by the studied cautiousness of the powers. But we are not afraid. Japanese propaganda has probably led American people to believe that Japanese troops have conquered great areas of our country. They have not. We are fighting them everywhere. Where flesh and blood, backed only by inferior arms, could not endure against great expenditure of explosives by the enemy, we have withdrawn, but we have not been defeated. Nor shall we be defeated if we are able to procure the means with which to equip ourselves. We are fighting and dying in defense of our soil, and for the principles that other nations profess to espouse; we only ask that those nations demonstrate clearly that there can be no fruits for the aggressor from this barbarous invasion and its monstrous inhumanities, and that the powers friendly to China and the Chinese people will take collective economic action to compel Japan to abandon her atrocious attempt to conquer our country.

6.

AN OPEN LETTER TO
ALMA MATER[3]

"Wellesley daughters in China will strive to uphold those splendid principles of life embodied in the inscription in bronze on the Palmer Memorial in our Chapel and written indelibly on our hearts by Wellesley tradition and teaching."

I HAVE before me your cablegram requesting a message. As you did not specify the nature of this message, I am somewhat at a loss to know what to send. To be sure, my class will have its twentieth reunion this year, and I am also the outside honorary member of the Class of 1938; therefore, perhaps, what you desire is a general greeting. Yet, when I consider Wellesley's passion for

[3] Madame Chiang Kai-shek graduated from Wellesley College, Massachussets, in 1917, being the first student from the Orient to be awarded the twin honors of the Wellesley and Durant scholarships. Early in 1938 Madame Chiang was voted an honorary member of the class of 1938.

[237]

social justice and service to our fellow men, as expressed in our motto, "Non ministrari sed ministare," and the fact that I have received numerous letters from Wellesley's daughters in every part of America, I am inclined to think that what you want is a statement of actual conditions now existing in China, and some idea of the bearing these problems should have on all who are intellectually honest and who earnestly desire to bring about a better world order. Whatever the future may bring to China, I want to thank all those who have expressed their sympathy for us, and who have stood loyally for those ideals for which China is now fighting. Also, I wish to assure our Alma Mater that her daughters in China will strive to uphold those splendid principles of life embodied in the inscription in bronze on the Palmer Memorial in our Chapel and written indelibly on our hearts by Wellesley tradition and teaching.

It is now twenty years since I left the Wellesley campus. As I write you this letter I am recalling the hopes, the dreams, the aspirations which fired us in our student days. America had then entered the World War. Most of my classmates had brothers, sweethearts, or friends fighting across the seas. All of us were busily occupied in our leisure time struggling with "knit four, purl two" and the intricacies of turning heels. How those nimble needles persevered! We were all so eager to do our bit to "make the world safe for democracy," to protect civilization, and to safeguard liberty. And we believed that such things could be done.

When I left America the armistice was not yet declared. War was adding to its horrors daily. But we clung to our high beliefs that the time had arrived when democracy and civilization could and would be saved from the further tortures of insensate carnage. Alas, for our high and innocent hopes. Two decades after the end of "that war to end all wars," I find myself involved in the throes of another excitement in expectation of another welter of blood and ruin.

Where now are our idealistic hopes? Where now stands the democracy we all thought we were helping so surely to save? Out of the terrible shadows which then made us shudder we were led to believe would come blessings for the salvation of humanity. No more, we thought, would youth grow up to be slain; no more would mothers weep over battlefields; no more would children be orphaned by the deadly fury of armed hate.

How tragically our dreams, our hopes, our beliefs have been torn to fragments by the futilities and the follies of mankind. Somehow I seem to hear caustic, ribald laughter somewhere — laughter at our innocence, or our foolishness, for democracy has not been saved but more endangered; and wars have not ended, but have become easier to launch and more deadly and destructive of human life and property.

Look at the terror-provoking inhumanities being perpetrated round about me — far and near in China — while I write. Here we have all those horrors of war I conjured up while at Wellesley magnified a thousandfold. Here is a war striking at the very heart of China. It is more ferocious, ruthless, and inhumane than can be described by any words I have in my vocabulary. It is an undeclared war, and, because it is an undeclared war, Japan has callously discarded all those international and human laws which were designed to protect noncombatants and neutrals in times of declared hostilities.

Great areas of my country have been ravaged and destroyed by air bombs, artillery, flames, and fury. My fellow countrymen have been slaughtered in cold blood by Japanese bombs and machine guns, by Japanese soldiers using bullets and bayonets against innocent people — killing able-bodied men, farmers, artisans, merchants — and violently outraging young girls and women. Wherever the Japanese army have gone they have left behind them charred and mutilated bodies, ruined homes, and blood-soaked earth. They have demolished by bomb and fire every school and college they have come across. Because they say they are hotbeds of resistance their first objectives are always the annihilation of institutes of learning.

This picture is no figment of imagination; no wartime atrocity story. It is stark and terrible reality — vouched for and verified by many of your own missionaries who have been eyewitnesses of these ghastly deeds. One American missionary told me that he saw with his own eyes Japanese soldiers line up hundreds of our able-bodied peasants who had taken refuge in the safety zone at Nanking, tie them together by the wrists in groups of fifty, and march them off to face firing squads manning machine guns and bayonets.

Another missionary told me that women and young girls who had taken refuge in missionary compounds were dragged out again and again by the Japanese military to be violated. In one compound in one night thirty-five different parties of Japanese soldiers entered the buildings and did their nefarious deeds. What happened to the women and girls in outlying country districts where they could not even have the protection of a foreign mission compound beggars imagination.

When the attention of the Japanese high command was drawn to these unspeakable brutalities and animalism they shrugged their shoulders. In time, they said, conditions would be better. But what has been the value of these promises? In areas the Japanese have now occupied for months no foreigner has been allowed to return to give aid to the wounded and the outraged, or to do any humane work. And why? Obviously because the Japanese authorities do not want eyewitnesses to observe and report the continued barbarities, or to expose their inability to discipline their soldiers.

I could go on endlessly recounting the shocking conditions now existing, but will spare you. Suffice it to say that this war has eclipsed all others for merciless mass murder, relentless ferocity, and despicable rapine.

The higher authorities of the Japanese army are not guiltless of what is now happening, because not only are they fully aware of the shocking horrors, but they themselves are actual participants in amazing organized national gangsterism which they naturally find vastly profitable. Everything with any intrinsic value has been taken, including furniture, iron and metalware, bed clothing, and even warm garments from the backs of the people. They have deliberately deprived the survivors of these terror-stricken regions of every means of livelihood in the hope that China shall perish. Consequently, we have now millions of refugees fleeing from one section of the country to another with their pitiful belongings under their arms or on their backs, dragging their children with them or losing them in the continuous assaults made upon them in their flight. Thousands of our children have been deported to Korea, Formosa, and Japan, to be brought up as future enemies of the Chinese race. The Japanese aim to train these children to hate everything Chinese, and to glorify only the Emperor of the Rising Sun. Tens of thousands of other children have been mercilessly slaughtered as part of Japan's criminal effort to destroy the future man power of China.

Swept by flames, deluged by blood, stripped by looters — you have a panorama of a ravaged, bleeding country.

And what is the purpose of this mass massacring; this meticulous marauding of China by the Japanese? Why this barbarism — this unleashing of unparalleled terror? It is inspired by the hope that they will be able to erect on the ashes of what was China a Japanese continental empire. An empire to dominate the Pacific, to have a determining voice in the foreign policies of Western nations, and to be, indeed, the overlord of the world.

For years past Japan has tried to lay the foundation for such a continental empire. She has defied the world, treaties, and international law. And now she is trying to "beat China to her knees," in fulfillment of the openly expressed threat of the Premier, Prince Konoye. She is wiping out in blood as much of the population of China as she can, and is hoping to demoralize surviving Chinese, their culture and civilization, by impoverishment and by the distribution wholesale of insidious narcotics. Read Muriel Lester's report to the League of Nations on her findings of what was happening in Manchuria when she investi-

gated conditions there. Similar infamies are being perpetrated in North China, and will follow in all occupied
regions.

Japan, finding that the Central Government's attitude
and its measures to warn our people against the narcotic
evil were making it difficult for her quickly to realize her
aims through demoralization by drugs, resorted to the
establishment of puppet regimes to secure control, and
the creation of "incidents" to justify armed aggression.

If Japan is allowed to have her way, and if she thus
wins the war, what will be the consequences? The Chinese
people who survive the barbarities will be so broken in
spirit that they will be unable to resist the will of the
invaders, for they will be beaten to impoverishment and
demoralization by the grossest inhumanities, and will become little better than slaves.

With Japan blockading our coast, we find it very difficult to secure equipment to continue our defense. In this
direction we surely should have help. I am not suggesting
that America, or anyone else, should go to war with Japan.
I am too much of a realist to believe that this would be
possible under present world conditions. But there are
other ways of restraining Japan and helping us. If they
are neglected, and if China should be defeated, not only
will China die, but foreign interests in the Far East will
also die in no uncertain time, and foreign commerce will

cease. The purchasing power of our surviving people will be completely destroyed by impoverishment, and America will lose the great potential market which, with our reorganization and national progress, we were developing when Japan decided to strike at us. You are a manufacturing country; you will have a great overflow of products, and China is the logical reservoir to take care of that overflow. The Chinese like American products, and each year, as our prosperity increased, we would naturally buy more and more of them, and automatically your prosperity would also increase.

If you look at America's export trade returns you will doubtless remark that, up to the present, America has been exporting more to Japan than to China. Undoubtedly true. But do you realize that if Japan once secures economic domination of China she will no longer require to buy American raw materials, your cotton, etc., or much of your manufactured articles? All these raw materials Japan could then have for the taking and, in time, she will make all that she will allow our people to possess.

But aside from the very material consideration which I have just mentioned, the fact is outstanding that if Japan conquers China she will become a world menace, because, with the exploitation of China's natural resources she will, in time, be able to secure the wherewithal to build great fleets, innumerable squadrons of bombing planes, and mobilize incalculable man power to harass your country as she is now harassing mine.

The conquering of China by Japan naturally connotes the eventual absorption by her of the Philippines and other tropical regions, not only to round off her hoped-for empire, but to make herself entirely independent of the products of temperate or tropical countries which she now has to import. That is the definite aim she is so persistently and so relentlessly pursuing. But it may never reach fulfillment, even if China has to carry on unaided.

Whatever may lie in the future, I doubt whether Japan will be able to conquer China. Her superior equipment and long-conceived military plans will have to reckon with the Spartan capacity of our people to endure suffering and their determination to struggle and to continue unrelenting resistance. Above all, there is the time-honored tenacity of purpose of our race, the infrangible influence of our philosophy, and the sustaining power of our culture, which have enabled us alone, as a nation, to survive through the centuries and overcome great national calamities such as floods, droughts, and epidemics, as well as years of fatuous civil warfare.

We are at present making great sacrifices and we are prepared to continue to sacrifice. These last ten years of reconstruction have not been in vain. Indeed, they have had galvanic effect upon our people. The Generalissimo had long recognized the fact that a trained army, as a physical unit, could not be effective if the masses did not understand the real meaning of nationalism. That is why we have, while making preparations for self-defense, spent most of our energy on rousing our people from the lethargic, inarticulate state into which they naturally drifted as a result of centuries of Manchu domination, oppression, and neglect. We have been trying to instill in our leaders a sense of what leadership involves — the responsibilities and the duties to the people — and, on the other hand, we have been stimulating the people to a realization of their responsibilities as citizens to the nation. And considering that we have had only a short time in which to try to offset the centuries of neglect and maladministration, we were making remarkable headway — by using the New Life Movement — with the program to develop mutual co-operation and good will between government officials and the people. The results were encouraging to us, but so disturbing to Japan that she decided that in order to succeed with her plans of conquest she had to strike before further progress could be made. It is insulting the world's intelligence for Japan to claim that she "loves" and wants to help the Chinese people, when all her actions exhibit her deliberate intention to destroy them and their progress.

I can hear you ask, what of our women, what are they

doing to help win this war? It is a long cry from "knitting socks for soldiers," as we did in college days, to the organizing of the work which the women of China are now doing. We are assiduously engaged in developing a Women's Movement. Women of every class, faction, and belief are now coming together to form a solid unit with the sole purpose of contributing what they can to the cause of the country. We are united as one. We have a definite program for training women behind the lines. Some of us have worked with the army as nurses; yes, some are shouldering rifles as soldiers. Look at "Old Mother Chao," that frail fifty-eight-year-old heroine, who hardly reaches above my shoulder, slipping in and out of the fighting lines, collecting funds for the ten thousand odd volunteers now harassing the enemy in North China, succoring the wounded, carrying messages to Army Headquarters, stimulating the morale of the guerrillas. She is invariably accompanied only by her youngest, sixteen-year-old daughter. Yesterday she told me that she and her four children had pledged not to desist in their efforts until our lost territory had been recovered, and that if any of them died none of the others would drop a useless tear of regret.

Think of that intrepid girl scout who braved the incessant fire of machine guns, the explosions of shells and bombs, and the danger of rifle bullets and bayonets to creep through the Japanese lines with our national flag for the "Battalion of Death" which preferred to fight to the death at Chapei, Shanghai, rather than surrender to the Japanese. She collected the last wills of those heroes and escaped through the enemy lines. She is now one of our most ardent workers in the cause of the refugee children. There are hundreds of other women and girls who are gladly giving themselves to the defense of our country. Still innumerable others are organizing the women in rural districts to conserve food and to do the work in the fields and factories formerly done by men. We have established a Refugee Children's Movement. We are gathering the war orphans of war-stricken areas and sending them into children's homes in the rear. Our immediate objective is to take care of twenty thousand children and, as time goes on, we shall care for as many as our resources will allow.

I have not shown you a very pretty picture of what is going on. It is, nevertheless, a true picture. I do not wish it to be disheartening. We, in China, are in high spirit. We will go on fighting as long as we can, and we hope victory will come to us.

What will come to the world we know not. It would seem that governments of civilized countries, by refraining from hazarding even a protest against the gross inhumanities that are exterminating thousands and ruining millions of noncombatants, are acquiescing in the abandonment of all modern and so-called civilized instruments to make war less cruel and ruthless, and are encouraging a return to barbarism. And it would, indeed, be strangely and pathetically ironic if the Chinese people, whose nation has survived centuries of world upheaval, transformation and tragedy, and all other changes that have rung down the long corridors of time, should reach this twentieth century period of so-called advanced civilization only to succumb, together with their age-old culture and civilization, to the annihilating devastation of advanced barbarism.

Those who are wisely realistic, who are intellectually honest, who have humane feelings in their hearts, will not hesitate for one moment to acknowledge that the future safety of the world depends upon the speed with which resolute restraining influences of some kind can be applied to those whose criminal infamies are now deluging my country with blood.

7.

OUR LOSS IS ALSO YOURS

*"With the destruction of our cultural centers
the world is losing a chance to enrich itself
through China's contributions to world thought."*

To MY mind there is an indissoluble bond between all
college students the world over. Their ideals cannot be
compassed by differences in language or distance, the en-
lightenment of education being universal. The Japanese
military have with calculated ferocity bombed all Chinese
educational institutions they could locate, claiming that
those institutions were hotbeds of resistance against Japanese efforts to dominate China. Consequently, tens of
thousands of students in China are now unable to continue
their studies. With the destruction of these cultural centers the world is losing a chance further to enrich itself
through the medium of Young China's social and progressive contributions to world thought. You will see that
our loss is also yours. Our educational institutions were
well on the way to develop certain lines of Eastern culture
which would supplement Western systems of education,

but now, with the destruction of our seats of learning, that effort has also been destroyed. It seems most fitting that the intellectuals whose tradition has always been to uphold freedom of thought and action are doing something definite to express not only disapproval but also condemnation of this manifestation of Japanese callousness, senseless brutality, and ruthlessness.

8.

YOUTH AND WORLD PEACE

"There is a call to youth to help save mankind from unprovoked, undeclared, aggressive warfare."

THE young people of this generation are fortunate to be born in an age remarkable for its scientific advancement. They are, too, in a way, decidedly unfortunate, because that very advancement compels us to face situations such as at present engulf China in ruin, and which threaten in turn to involve the world.

It was hoped that the Great War would be the last of international armed conflicts. Unhappily, the aftermath of that war developed conditions which have inexorably led to a situation even worse than existed before world peace crashed in 1914.

We, in China, are now suffering tragically from that new device of the barbaric-minded called "undeclared warfare." The bombing planes of Japan are flying all over our country drenching it with death and destruction. They have been doing it for months past. What they fail to accomplish in the way of annihilation is completed, when possible, by their soldiers. Consequently, we are witnessing in operation in China a system of slaughter and ruin which ignores those human rights hitherto protected by international agreement of some kind or other.

This generation, when it matures, is, therefore, going to be burdened with tremendous risks and responsibilities. That is not the fault of their elders, however. It is a consequence of the development in the world of new political ideas, and the manner of their enforcement may be ascribed definitely to the influence of the Great War upon the minds of certain men who were soldiers in that war and who now find themselves hoisted by the whirligig of time into a position enabling them personally to invoke the ruthless employment of force to fulfill ambitions of their own for power, or to secure territorial expansion for their countries. Because of this the wise youth of today are compelled by the very force of circumstances to apply themselves with unprejudiced and open minds to a study of world conditions so that they may discover what lies ahead of them, and so that they may equip themselves to meet dangers greater than any that faced their fathers or their grandfathers.

War is a terrible agency, and modern inventions have made it cataclysmic in its potentialities, especially when employed in ruthless defiance of such instruments as treaties and laws, which were specially designed eventually to

end wars and to safeguard human life. The sufferings of
the world which have been caused by the follies of this
kind of fighting are right before us for study. It behooves
everyone to try to learn and appreciate just what have
been the causes of this suffering, what produced present
conditions in China, and what the effects will be in time
if restraint is not imposed where it should be—that is, in
the first place, upon Japan. The tragic aggression on
China, with its infamies and horrors, can be repeated in
America or in other countries, quite easily now that the
conquest of the air is advancing so rapidly. Also, the
progress of science and invention generally, or, perhaps,
the use of some South American state or other, can make
invasion of the United States possible.

Unless the aggressive peoples are taught, beyond
doubt, that a high sense of justice prevails in the democratic world; that humane sentiments are paramount;
that respect for treaties and international agreements is
unshakably and unalterably part and parcel of the foundations of democracies, and that countries violating those
principles will be instantly barred from the family of
decent nations, it is easy to foresee now what use the
products of advanced science may be put to in the Amer-
icas when the time is judged to be propitious.

I can only hope that the youth of today will really become the wise men of tomorrow.

9.

SPIRITUAL MOBILIZATION

OF MY COUNTRY

*"Out of the ashes which the Japanese are
spreading all over our country will arise
a phoenix of great national worth."*

THE purpose of the inauguration of the Ching Shen
Chung Tung Yuan (People's Spiritual Mobilization) is
of vital national consequence. It is to stimulate and intensify public interest and active participation in three
major national requirements: the practical application of
the tenets of the New Life Movement; the continuance
of resolute and unfaltering resistance against the Japanese invaders; the planning of realistic measures for reconstruction and rehabilitation in the vast areas that have
been deliberately laid waste by the Japanese.

The officials and people of our suffering country are
being urged to rise together to higher heights of philosophy, patriotism, unselfishness, courage, endurance, and

generosity with but one national aim: that out of the agonizing sufferings and losses that have been brought upon us we shall arise a new people.

Our enemies have boasted that they intend to beat us to our knees and break our spirit. We shall show them, as we shall show our friends, that in the blood of our fellow men and the ashes of our burned homes has flowered a new national spirit.

We shall show them that the new China that was in the making, before war was invoked to destroy it, is still marching on — wiser, more patriotic, unafraid. We Chinese, in our long history, have survived great natural and political calamities; we have triumphed over prolonged adversity, and we have carried our culture and civilization and our national entity safely through the ages no matter what nations rose or fell about us. What our inherent powers of endurance, philosophy, and patience have enabled us to do in the past they will fortify us to do in the present as in the future.

What we have to do, and what we are going to do, is to carry on. By applying with intensity of purpose the principles of the New Life Movement we shall go far. We must develop to the fullest extent the advantages of co-operation in carrying out the responsibilities of citizenship and of mutual help in solving our social and national problems. Time has proved that we possess the stamina and the character to face prolonged trials and tribulations, and we shall not fail now.

The New Life Movement, when it was launched, was welcomed by our people, for the practical and spiritual help it gives. The political unity that also came to our country in 1936 was accepted with pride and gratitude as the prelude to permanent peace and prosperity. Reform was appearing everywhere. Interprovincial jealousies had disappeared with the widespread development of inter-provincial communications. Out of disorder emerged the substantial beginnings of definite co-operation in political, social, and economic spheres. We were well justified in the belief that at last the well-being of our people was a foremost concern of our government, and that unimpeded progress would be our lot in both domestic and international affairs.

But as a snake strikes at its unsuspecting prey, so struck Japan at us, and our hope of peace was crushed. Unrestrained fury and hate were loosed upon us. We fought back, unprepared as we were, because there was nothing else left for us to do. We are still fighting back. We must do so, or submit to slavery as a people and death as a nation.

We must fight, as every self-respecting nation must fight, because our country is being violated; because millions of our people have been put to flight, sacrificing their all, by fear of death; because hundreds of thousands of our helpless men, women, and children have been slaughtered in agony, by bombs, by bullets, and by bayonets; because thousands of our unfortunate girls and women have been violently and shockingly outraged; because personal and public property valued at billions of dollars has been wantonly demolished in villages, towns, and cities; because the most outrageous organized rapine the world has ever seen is being engaged in with the sinister object of destroying the means of livelihood of our survivors, as well as enriching the uniformed looters of Japan. It is the most gigantic spectacle of shameless wholesale robbery ever seen.

The refugee problem is an immense and increasing one. As the vast homeless masses struggle into one district or another, each district finds its difficulties increased by just as many refugees as arrive there after saturation point has been reached. Agricultural areas are able, quietly and without ostentation, to absorb great numbers, but the hungry and helpless masses always on the march must be taken care of. System and order are required to deal with the situation, and benefit or charity organizations must cooperate and interlace, rather than overlap, in order effectively to meet the terrible situation.

We are faced now with great responsibilities, and I am sure that they will be taken up with a will, and that courage and resoluteness will both come to the front and help us save our fellow citizens and our nation. Calamity such as ours calls for special qualities if it is to be overcome successfully. Not only must we have the courage to face our enemy, but we must have the courage to face the hitherto peaceful and industrious population of region upon region being folded back upon us by relentless invasion and thus increasing our burdens as well as testing our capabilities and our patriotism.

Indeed, to be able to do justice to ourselves and materially cope with the situation we need not only physical and moral courage, but we need the wisdom and strength of will to abandon all selfishness that may be part of us. What is called for now is the highest type of unquestioned co-operation, and the readiness to do everything helpful to which we can put our hands. There is no room now for personal pride, or individual irritations, or doubts. There must be unified confidence in developing the means to one end, and that end is our national salvation and progress.

Out of this great peril and trial may come great harm to China, or great blessings. Failure intelligently to cope with the task that lies before us might bring future chaos; but if we handle our responsibilities successfully nothing but national victory can result, even if we have to pay for it in years of further agony and blood.

This war has been forced upon us, and the terrible

slaughter of human beings has been permitted for some inscrutable reason. Let us feel that it is to shake our nation out of its apparent lethargy, out of what has been believed to be inherent indifference. There used to be provincial differences which kept our country distraught, but they have been broken down not only by the political unity that came to China, and by the highways that opened provincial communication, but by the war that we are now fighting. Not only are troops of all provinces fighting together, but now people of all provinces are working together, and many, unhappily, are fugitives together in one strange province or another.

What this melting of differences in dialect, opinion, and feelings may do for China can be appreciated by anyone with imagination, hope, and constructive energy. Out of the ashes which the Japanese are spreading all over our country will spring a phoenix of great national worth if we so will it. And if we, by determination, pull together and strive in every way possible to sustain our armies to resist our foes, and to help those who are suffering among us, we will surely see our country freed from the invaders. We can make a new China if we now make up our minds to work together, to be resolute in the performance of our tasks, and to be courageous in facing the main objective to defeat the enemy.

There are many problems for us to solve, but reconstruction is one requiring the deepest thought and wisest planning. Involved in this problem is one which will be of first magnitude in the future—the demobilization of the soldiers. That in itself is a stupendous task for any country, but for China, being burnt out as she is by the Japanese, it is going to prove one of great concern and difficulty to all who have responsibility for coping with it. While the war is certain to be of long duration, we still must make plans for dealing with the situation at the end of it, and if the refugee problem is capably dealt with now that will contribute largely to the competent settlement of others.

I feel that the women of China will, on their part, be inspired to apply themselves with wisdom and bravery to the handling of the unfortunate homeless masses, especially the children, and I am convinced that all sections of our people will be resolute to endure and to make sacrifices. The intellectuals, in particular, have the opportunity of displaying qualities of leadership which should be a stimulating contribution to all connected with the organization of national resistance upon an effective basis. They can help in many ways, in organizing the people, and in assisting guerrilla units. There is room everywhere for intelligent leadership particularly in developing farming and industry.

We must grow more and more foodstuffs of all kinds;

we must give of our means and our labor. Do that and we will encourage others. And we will inspire our friends and well-wishers in foreign countries to lend us a continuous hand in the finding of the great sums of money that will be vitally necessary to provide for the millions who are being deliberately deprived of their resources and will be thrown upon charity, not only of surviving Chinese able to take their part, but upon that of the world at large.

Japan, owing to circumstances, is able to perpetrate the grossest inhumanities in our country in defiance of international law. To the world this contribution to chaos by Japan is terrifying, but we must stand up to it, and do our best to achieve victory.

While we Chinese are unable to accept blame, or take responsibility, for the consequences arising from the callous abrogation of international laws by Japan, we are confronted by the sufferings they develop, and it is our duty not only to continue courageously defending our country but at the same time, with undaunted spirit, to assist in the solution of the problems connected with that suffering.

The apparent acceptance by the governments of first-class powers of the infamous conduct of the Japanese army in violation of humane and other laws has bewildered large sections of our people. Many are more bewildered

CHINA IN WARTIME

by the failure of those governments to attempt even to protect their own interests by collectively moving in such a way as to compel Japan to abandon her brutalities. There are understandable reasons why they have not been able to do anything, but disappointing as the attitude of the governments has been, it is clear that the terrible trials and sufferings of our people have deeply horrified the people of the civilized world. That is a comforting and consoling thing. In particular the people of Great Britain and the British Dominions and America, are, of their own volition, recording their condemnation of Japan's criminal debaucheries in our country. They are also testifying their practical sympathy with us by sending medical aid and money to help us in the great humane work of overcoming the consequences of the colossal calamity that has come upon us.

I have personally received many hundreds of letters from all kinds of people living in various countries, condoling with us, encouraging us, praying for us. The depth of expression shown in all these letters, the abiding faith in all of them that we will be victorious, is inspiring and deeply moving. The people of the great democracies are doing what they can to help us in our woe; and it is certain that they will, if they can, do more as time goes on.

What our foreign friends and sympathizers are doing deserves, and I am sure will earn, our eternal gratitude.

At the same time it is a direct challenge to us to go on fighting our own battle, and to intensify the work that has already been undertaken here for the amelioration of the lot of the survivors.

With our civilians courageously taking up their burdens the armed forces will be more and more tenacious in their efforts to win to victory. Close co-operation between all who can help will profoundly influence the course of events to victory and to the ultimate glorification of our country.

Unhappily the impoverished Chinese millions will require more help than will be available in China. Organized help should come from governments abroad, not only from the sympathetic people, because of the danger of the loss of this great potential market. With the deliberate widespread ruin being inflicted by the Japanese, and with the loss of means of livelihood of the survivors in ravaged regions, there will be dire poverty. That will lead to complete loss of purchasing and producing power until the future restores normal conditions. Without return to production there can be no commerce, and no commerce will close China indefinitely to the trading people of foreign countries.

That is, of course, why Japan launched her relentless campaign and why Japanese officers and soldiers are deliberately following their looting of occupied territory. It is this criminal marauding, on a scale never before seen, or permitted by civilized nations, that is going to intensify Chinese poverty, cramp the world's commerce, and aggravate the difficulties of settling the masses of roaming refugees and finding means of subsistence for demobilized soldiers, unless something is done now by the governments of the democracies.

The tragedy of China, if she is unable to overcome the barbaric onslaught being made upon her, will be that she, alone of all nations, has survived many centuries of world upheavals, has triumphed over great natural calamities and internal wars, has successfully carried her culture and her civilization through the vicissitudes of countless generations, only to lose it now when civilization is supposed to be at its zenith, when the world is supposed to have long abandoned barbarism and duplicity and hedged itself in with wisely realistic treaties and laws so as to make the life of the individual, the community, and the nation, peaceful, prosperous, and secure.

10.

THE "WARPHANS"

"We hear little children cry, 'Father, mother, do not leave me behind. I won't cry any more.'"

As you will realize, if you look at the map of China, this war is covering a tremendous territory. Refugees are being driven from areas over hundreds of thousands of square miles. The children have to be collected, as best we can, throughout this vast region. They are first taken to centers and are then passed on to various institutions, official and missionary, in the rear.

Briefly, the following is the process: We send people out to the various war areas to try to collect the children, but oftentimes we gather them from the roadsides in districts which have been bombed.

Families fleeing from war areas to the rear usually have four or five children. They have to traverse great distances. As transportation is so difficult on all sides we hear little children cry, "Father, mother, do not leave me behind. I won't cry any more."

Often a family starts out with several children. When they reach their destination only one or two may be left, because the parents have neither the money nor the physical strength to continue caring for them. These people at one time were fairly well to do, otherwise they never could have started on the long trek and escaped from the war zones.

As a first step, we have undertaken to care for twenty-thousand children. So far, in every province in the rear we have established orphan homes. The workers are usually volunteers. All workers who devote full time to the care of the children are given board and lodging, and an allowance of $3 (U. S. currency) per month. This rate of remuneration ensures that only those genuinely interested in children will apply. Overhead expenses are thus cut to the bone.

We have a National Committee which looks after the refugee children. This committee is divided into subcommittees whose work consists of gathering the children, transporting them, and placing them in the rear, for eventual adoption by private individuals or families, or for care in mission or government institutions. All committee members, whether national or local, give their services free.

Every cent contributed goes directly to the National Committee which, in turn, sees to it that the funds are used directly for the care and education of the orphans and children of poor refugees. The cost for housing, clothing, and educating each child has been worked out at $20 (U. S. currency) per year.

The first group of refugee children consisted of more

than five hundred, collected in Kaifeng, Honan Province. Other children who have been collected have come from Anhwei Province, where Luan is the largest station, and along the Lung-Hai front, which includes the large stations of Hsuchow, in Kiangsu Province; Kaifeng and Chengchow, in Honan Province.

The refugees are concentrated at these large stations from the surrounding country and from interior points. Our first task is to try to ascertain which children are true orphans and which are foundlings. Many, if not most, of the surviving children have either father or mother living, but have lost contact with them. In many cases parents send their children to be taken care of by the refugee centers as they have no means of supporting them. Otherwise they would die of starvation.

The children sent to the centers by their parents are taken in on condition that the parents sign an agreement stating that they wish the refugee center to raise the children to prevent their being abandoned. The name, record, and history of the child are registered.

At first the adult refugees did not understand the reason for collecting the children, and believed the action was not to their benefit. But later they learned that the children were being taken to the rear of the battle lines to be cared for. Then refugees began to pour into the centers to register and to send in their children.

For the collection of the first group, twenty-four members of the Relief Association, among whom were some members of the Board of Directors, were sent to Kaifeng. The children were transported to Hankow in groups of two and three hundred. The War Area Service Corps aids in the collection of children in the war areas. There are altogether five war zones. In each zone we have established receiving centers. Catholic and Protestant missions in all localities give continuous help.

Upon arrival at the central clearing station the children are washed, dressed in clean clothing, and each one undergoes a physical examination. Each child is given a number and a tag, and its name is registered. Most of the children are found to be in good health. Their ages range from three to fourteen years, but also many newly-born babies, who have been abandoned, are being cared for. The children collected are mostly boys, few girls being found.

The children are taught what is termed "wartime education." It consists of learning to recognize written characters, to be patriotic, etc., and resembles the regular primary education. At their permanent homes they will be given vocational training such as agriculture, manual work, making sandals, towels, and so on.

Where the different foreign missions are helping the Relief Association to care for the children in their institutions, the association finances the care of the children but the mission supplies the staff, the missions being established organizations. Also, the missions at this time are not carrying on their usual schoolwork and, consequently, have the space to accommodate the refugee children.

The distribution of the children on June 1, 1938, was as follows:

Name of Place	Number of children already received	Organization
Chiaokow, Hupeh Province	100	London Mission
Chingshan " "	50	American Church Mission
Huangchow " "	50	Swedish Mission
Ichang, " "	150	American Church Mission
Tayeh, " "	100	Methodist Mission
Szekiang, Hunan "	50	Famine Orphanages and Evangelistic Band
Kaifeng, Honan "	2,000	Catholic Mission
Station on Kiangsi Border	500	Women's Relief Association
Kuling, Kiangsi Province	100	Women's Relief Association
Kiukiang, " "	100	Danforth Memorial Hospital
Chungking, Szechwan "	1,000	Women's Relief Association
Chengtu, Szechwan "	1,000	Women's Relief Association
Kweilin, Kwangsi "	500	Women's Relief Association
Kweiyang, Kweichow "	1,000	Women's Relief Association
Hongkong	2,000	Women's Relief Association
Canton, Kwangtung "	Transients	Women's Relief Association
Foochow, Fukien " "		Women's Relief Association
Hankow, Hupeh " "		Women's Relief Association
Chekiang Province	1,000	Women's Relief Association
Nanchang, Kiangsi "	1,000	Women's Relief Association

These are all the details I am able to give at present. I am actively perfecting the organization. I am hopeful that when the children are settled down at permanent places we will be able, as a matter of interest, to let the little waifs know who are helping to support them. This will, of necessity, be a bit complicated, but I hope to simplify it in course of time through registration and photographs.

Remember that $20 covers upkeep for only one year. It is possible that many of the children will have to be kept in orphanages until they grow up. We are hopeful of distributing as many as possible among Chinese families in various parts of the country soon after hostilities cease.

But when will hostilities cease? And when they do cease, what will be the condition of the country? Will there be sufficient families well enough off properly to care for additional members of their families? The whole social system will be shaken from its foundations, and it will be a long time for those foundations to be re-established. When this aspect of war is considered it may be realized what are the terrible consequences of the wide-spread devastation and demolition being systematically carried out by the Japanese.

That problem has a great bearing on the future of the refugees. The refugees are people who have been driven by war out of the regions where their ancestors have lived and died. And when the war is over, they expect, as is their right, to return and reoccupy those lands and what is left of their homes. Is there not an international body that is going to see to it that gigantic robbery of the type now being instituted is prevented? If not, we do not know what will become of the millions of refugees who will have been thus deprived of their possessions.

Even if we have to move out of Hankow, a look at the map will show how much other country there is for us to fight in. So, friends of China who cannot help her in her fighting should not be disappointed when we move; that is the only strategy we can adopt against the heavy equipment of the Japanese. But, the further inland we go the more losses the Japanese are going to sustain in men and money. We are certain that we can hold on no matter how long the war lasts, providing we can get supplies of munitions and equipment.

Unhappily, as the war goes on we also lose. Greater areas of our country are overrun and the problem of the refugees and the children becomes more acute. Because of this, and because friendly countries cannot materially help us in our fighting, we hope they will help us in this humanitarian work which must be carried on if millions of people are not to die in their tracks from starvation. The greatest mass movement ever known in history is taking place in China, and it is rendered possible only by the breakdown of treaties and international law.

II.

MOTHERS OF CHINA

"While our hearts are full of admiration for the heroism of our troops there is an abiding pride in the mothers who have had to sacrifice their sons."

WHILE we are all gratified over the recent victories of our troops on all fronts, and our hearts are full of admiration for their splendid courage and heroism, there is poignant grief for those in all sections of society who have been killed during the war, and abiding pride in the mothers who have had to suffer and sacrifice their sons.

The sufferings of our people and the sacrifices of our troops have been so intense and unprecedented that it is difficult to find words sufficiently expressive to depict the agonies the nation has undergone during the recent months. Yet how infinitely more intense have been the mental tortures of the mothers who, along with their own physical pains brought about by hostilities, have had to bear the added knowledge of the agonies that have been inflicted upon their sons and daughters.

From time immemorial Chinese mothers have given themselves to the upbringing of their children for the welfare of the nation. Mencius, Er Yang Hsiu, Fan Jung Yi, and Yo Fei are some of the outstanding examples. The mothers of all those national heroes were widowed in early life, and, despite poverty and uncontrollable vicissitudes, brought up their sons to become great men.

We are all familiar with the story of how the mother of Mencius, having realized the importance that environment plays in the development of character, persisted in moving from place to place until she found one which would have a favorable influence upon the boy.

Er Yang Hsiu and Fan Jung Yi both became premiers during the Sung dynasty. Er Yang Hsiu's mother was so poor that she had no money to buy either paper, ink or brush, but, being a resourceful woman, she overcame circumstances and used a reed as a pen to write on the sand to instruct her boy. This is how we come to have the story of "drawing with a reed to instruct the son." Also, through the personal teachings and influence of his mother during his childhood, Fan Jung Yi — when he became premier — formulated and carried out the philosophical principles in his famous self-admonition: "The first to be troubled over the sorrows under the heavens; the last to enjoy the blessings," which finally brought prosperity and happiness to the people.

The phrase illustrating a frugal life: "Portion out the salt vegetables, divide the rice gruel," indicates how Fan, as a young student, limited his intake of food to the minimum amount necessary for sustenance, because he remembered his mother's economical habits during her struggle for livelihood during his infancy. The story is known to every school child.

Yo Fei's mother inculcated in her son the principles of undying devotion and loyalty to the country by tattooing on his back the following characters: "Utmost loyalty to recompense the country." And because of this she is perhaps most revered by our people as an example of an outstanding patriotic mother.

Coming to the present day, there is the example of "Old Mother Chao," that courageous heroine whose fine, unquenchable spirit, albeit in so frail a body, conquers all physical handicaps. She travels incessantly, going from place to place, making contacts for the volunteers in North China and securing contributions for their support. She not only has given her whole soul to this work of helping the defenders of our country, but she has also inspired and dedicated all her children to the same cause.

She has given everything she possesses in this world to this objective. More than this, she has given us a striking, modern example of courageous devotion to the country which a mother can set for her children. She is but one of the many mothers who have dedicated themselves with equal fervor to the defense of our soil. There are countless other mothers in China today who have decided that they prefer to see their children dead rather than become slaves of Japanese aggressors.

The qualities distinguishing these mothers I have mentioned point to the reasons for the greatness inherent in our Chinese race, and the potentialities for further development in the future of our nation.

Their philosophy of life; their calm acceptance of existing conditions as a basis upon which to build their hopes; their ability to meet every emergency by making use of resources at hand; their refusal to surrender in the face of seemingly insurmountable obstacles; their sublime faith in the ultimate outcome of their aspirations; their fortitude and courage to battle against adversities so that they might translate their faith into living reality; the deep reservoir of their silent strength to carry out their appointed tasks, and their tenacity of purpose — all these characteristics are not confined to them alone, but are possessed by all Chinese mothers in a greater or less degree. The *Book of Odes* makes numerous references to the high spiritual status of mothers.

To our own mothers we all owe an unpayable debt. The mothers of most of us may not be so spectacular nor may their renown be so great, but the typical and average Chinese mother is the embodiment of the virtues of our race.

Many of our mothers have already passed away, but

their memories are forever enshrined in our hearts. We remember the innumerable sacrifices they have made on our behalf, their ever-ready sympathy and protecting love, and their gentle patience with our youthful waywardness.

Therefore, I make a special plea that we cherish and honor all mothers whether they are alive or whether they exist only in our hearts and memories; and that to the wisdom, the goodness, the self-sacrifice, the courage, and the fortitude of these mothers we pay our respectful homage.

12.

JAPAN'S CONTINENTAL POLICY

A PERIL TO THE WORLD

"International peace can only come through mutual respect; through mutual observance of treaties, law, and agreements; and through nations collectively acting to discipline anyone that defaults."

JAPAN began the invasion of China on July 7, 1937, and after months of effort has failed to realize her first requirement for success. Instead of the Chinese forces failing to resist the aggression, they have surprised the Japanese, and the world, by fighting so resolutely that the Japanese have been compelled, by this time of writing,[1] to send to China vast reinforcements of men and munitions to recover the position of professed superiority which they have lost to Chinese inferior arms and equipment.

If the past months can be regarded as the first stage of

[1] May, 1938.

[283]

the war, Japan has so far signally failed. She boasted that one Japanese soldier was equal to any ten Chinese soldiers; she claimed that within three months the war would be over so far as she was concerned, and that all she required in China would be at her disposal. She even went ahead, it seems, not only counting the chickens before they were hatched, but preparing the coops to confine them. People of the outside world seem to have been surprised at what China has done, probably because they have little knowledge of the change that has been taking place in this country during the past few years, and have accepted the Japanese estimate of conditions in China, as well as Japan's opinion of her own military competence and invincibility. But Occidental people are not alone in their lack of knowledge of what has been going on in China, or the failure correctly to appraise it. The Japanese themselves have shown lamentable ignorance of the depth and extent of the fundamental spiritual change which has been at work among the Chinese people.

The Japanese were aware that unity was coming to China, however, and they did not like it. They realized, too, that there were some changes pending that would prove of great detriment to their ambitions if permitted to develop without interruption. It was the fear that these changes would produce reorganization and consolidation that prompted the Japanese to take immediate action. To ensure a proper understanding of the situation it must be pointed out that for years the Japanese have left no stone unturned to keep China disunited and disorganized. They have always hoped that they would be able to achieve a position of dominance on the continent which would enable them to monopolize the exploitation of the natural resources and labor of the country without any difficulty. Eventual control, they considered, would then be easy, and a Japanese continental empire could certainly be established. Their dreams have not been confined solely to China. They have, for a long period, visualized the banners of Japan waving over the whole of Asia. Count Tanaka, in his notorious memorandum of some years ago, detailed the essential measures to be taken for the translation of that dream into realistic fact, and the militarists of Japan have followed his program with the tenacity of insatiable zealots. The present ferocious campaign of conquest is a part of the long-premeditated plan.

To facilitate their progress toward this glittering goal the Japanese have for years endeavored to convince the people of the world that China was chaotic, incompetent, and incorrigible, and badly in need of a stern, disciplinarian hand. Their propaganda was designed to influence the Occidental mind to accept the Japanese as the divinely appointed Draco, and to allow them free and unquestioned scope in China to quiet the alleged chronic turbulence and to initiate a peaceful administration in accordance with their plans as arbiters of Far Eastern affairs.

It is regrettable to have to say that it appears as though many foreign countries accepted the Japanese propaganda at its face value, irrespective of the lesson that should have been taught by Japan's unscrupulous invasion and occupation of Manchuria. Otherwise, how can apparent international acquiescence in Japan's unbridled ruthlessness be explained?

The foreign mind has been influenced, it must be supposed, to doubt China because of the long period of civil wars and because of the efforts on the part of deposed, disgruntled militarists to recover the positions and power from which they had been ejected. Probably it was not realized by foreigners abroad that Japanese agents were behind much of the rebellion and internecine warfare, just as they are busy trying to create puppet states now. Then, too, there was the attitude of mind of many foreigners in China who had no patience with the growing pains of the country during its transition from the ancient monarchical autocracy of the Manchus to a modern republican form of government. Foreign merchants, in particular, had the misfortune to suffer from dislocation of commerce within the country. This they resented; and, perhaps, what they resented more was their inability to acquire the easy fortunes that marked the expansive prerevolutionary times—mourned now as the "good old days"—when concession hunting was a kind of speculative indoor sport, and competition in trade was not so keen, while in some lines it was rendered comparatively insignificant by the Chinese consumer's stubborn loyalty to an established trademark.

The foreign merchants were so wedded to the system that existed in those times that they disliked, or were unwilling, to undertake the brain fag or the physical exertion required by an effort to get out of their old grooves and to adjust themselves to the new order which was destined to develop in China. In fact, they did not foresee successful radical changes, or even believe such were possible. On the other hand, those foreigners who were sympathetic with the struggles of China did realize that portentous changes were on the way in the country. They were able to visualize a China casting off its shackles and marching briskly along the democratic highway to the drumbeats of modernized progress, developing unity, improving administration, and expanding communications. They could see that, in time, the establishment of peace and order would bring close upon its heels systematic economic improvement which would cause a striking rise in the standard of living of the people, a consequent increase in their purchasing power, and a concurrent growth in their demands for the products of Western nations. But this handful of informed foreigners had no influence upon the inveterate suspicion of all things Chinese entertained by the bulk of their disappointed compatriots. These so-called "die-hards" could not admit that China had any right at all to change, although political upheavals have marked the history of many Western nations.

So this "undeclared" war broke out with little understanding of it in the mind of the average world citizen. All the efforts that were being made to promote the well-being of the Chinese people and open up their country were either unrealized by the average foreigner or were forgotten. Also, they were promptly threatened by the invasion. Further confusion was added when Japanese leaders swamped the world with broadcasts of Japan's "justification" for taking steps to "spank" the "outrageous Chinese," and to make "peace" in Asia. The Japanese did not possess the intellectual honesty to add that they had previously threatened China with dire calamity if she pursued her traditional friendship with Great Britain or America, nor did they recall that they had notified those countries that their assistance to put China on her feet was none of their business, but was the special province of Japan alone.

The outcome of this war, no matter what it may be, will have far-reaching consequences to the whole world. More important, it will have direct, as well as indirect, influence particularly upon the national and commercial future of Great Britain and the people of the British Dominions. If Japan is victorious—which she cannot be unless the democracies assist her to overwhelm China by refusing to give China financial facilities to acquire the equipment and munitions necessary for self-defense—the menace to the British possessions will grow rapidly.

Japan will have under her control the vast resources of China to build up her fighting forces, and with these she will set about the fulfillment of her ambition to bring all Oriental peoples under her sway in pursuance of her Pan-Asiatic policy. India will be sure to fall, because of the very incongruous texture of its peoples. And the rounding off of Japan's continental empire will involve the acquisition not only of China and Siberia east of longitude 110°, but also of all the land east of that longitude from latitude 20° north to 50° south, which means, of course, the Philippines, East Indies, the Pacific Islands, and Australasia. Fanciful, you think? So was the attempt to bite off Manchuria (but it succeeded so far as the world is concerned); so is the present effort to swallow China; so did it appear impossible for Japan to overthrow with one fell blow the complex machinery built through generations of time purposely to sustain civilization, control war, and protect civilian populations from death, rape, and rapine.

Yet treaties and international laws have been contemptuously disregarded, and Japan has put in their place the system of "undeclared" war and its horrors by which China, for a second time, is being victimized.

What is being done in China today can, unless the democracies beware, be done in any of the British possessions tomorrow.

The acceptance of "undeclared" warfare as being within the realm of practical politics is pregnant with acute danger everywhere. Humanitarianism is tossed to the winds, hope in justice is fast disappearing. The prestige of those great civilized nations who profess to be champions of ethics in international dealings will also disappear into the limbo. If it is only fear of Japan that prompts Occidental nations to maintain silence, they had better so inform Japan and, incidentally, other countries, for Japan is pursuing its policy of drenching China in blood and reducing it to a scorched wilderness, firm in the belief that the Occidentals have forgotten their professed principles and are ready to accept the new order of things as a product of the changing times. It must be fear, of course, or there would not be this frantic burdening of the people with mounting taxation for towering armaments. When we, in China, see these vast expenditures it is natural for us to wonder why the nations concerned do not indulge in a little mental arithmetic to see how much they would ulti-

mately save if they aided China now in her effort to bring
to her senses the author of this new terror.

At the head and front of contemptuous jettisoning of
treaties and international law stands Japan. China was the
first victim and Japan, because she was unchecked by the
world, is once again expending her mighty wrath upon
us. We had the temerity, or the audacity, to try to defend
ourselves, and that outraged her. While we ask for justice,
it must be said that the democratic powers, if anything,
owe definite assistance to China, and no deference of any
kind to Japan — that is, if they are true to their principles.

It seems that by providing China with the means to
continue her defense, the democratic nations would not
only be vindicating their beliefs and upholding their principles, but they would be saving colossal sums which
they must sink in armaments, eventually particularly to
fight the very power that has been responsible for the
world upheavals and has been trying for months past to
conquer China and eliminate all foreign interests in China.
Whether or not we are helped honorably, as we should
be, we shall continue fighting, and we hope we shall meet
with success similar to that which has so far attended us.

I wonder if Western people realize what is happening
here. For their information, the so-called invincible army
of Japan, which the Premier, Prince Konoye, threatened
was going to beat us to our knees in no time, has been

constrained not only to revise its ideas but also to augment itself continuously with reinforcements, until last month it had thirty divisions, totaling six hundred thousand men, operating in China, with the whole nation now mobilized on a war footing. The cost to her of all this enterprise in "making friends of the Chinese people" can be estimated by using as a basis the per diem cost of the Great War, or by watching Japan's appropriations. Yet this full-dress war is but an "incident," according to Japanese army professions, though to their people at home it will soon reveal itself as a monstrous major calamity, launched without justification and continuing without benefit to anyone except the providers of equipment and munitions. And there is the tragedy.

The longer, therefore, that the obsessed militarists of Japan are enabled to continue with their ruthless destruction the worse it will be for China and for the whole world. Not only will "undeclared" warfare become sanctified by custom, but this potential market will be ruined for many years for the industrial and commercial peoples of other nations.

We shall, however, go on fighting as long as we can secure anything to fight with. We know, and the Japanese now know to their sorrow, what guerrilla warfare is. How these guerrillas have been disillusioned regarding certain beliefs about Japan is illustrated by the experience of farmers in Shansi Province, who had formed guerrilla bands to protect their womenfolk and their farms. They have discovered, to their simple astonishment—so I have been informed by a foreigner who lives in that region—a phenomenon they believed impossible of proof: that a bullet from a blunderbuss, or a stab by a pike, can kill a sacred and invincible Japanese soldier in hand-to-hand combat just as easily and effectively as either can destroy any ordinary small-time bandit or badman; that a hole in a highway can upset a Japanese truck or tank, even though flying a dozen supernatural flags, just as it can upturn a homely ricksha or rickety-wheeled mulecart, if the hole is artistically camouflaged. This great discovery has suddenly exploded a lot of myths about the Japanese in the interior of our land; has robbed the Japanese, as man to man, of their terror to our soldiers, and it is, in reality, the simple and honest explanation of the unexpected failure of the Japanese army to fulfill its boasts, and of the plight in which the Japanese forces find themselves, in all parts of China, despite the overwhelming weight of artillery and tanks and mechanized units.

Military observers are well aware of all of this, and should be able to estimate the real value of Japanese military, air, and naval might if it is challenged by any first-class power. Curiously, however, it is Japan that has always been doing the challenging, and it is the democracies, just like despised China, which have always been reluctant to answer her back. Is it not true that fear of Japan by other nations has been bred of exactly the same stuff as that which held our own people in awe of them, until we discovered that they are no more immune to injury than are we, and that their "invincibility," and hopes of victory, depend more upon the efficient use of modern death-dealing inventions than upon the effectiveness of brains or brawn? Courage alone is not a monopoly of Japanese soldiers, and they have disclosed, by their terrible actions, that discipline is no more characteristic of them than it was of the savages of old. The very unrestrained employment of the grossest barbarism to terrorize and demoralize our people was a preliminary confession by the Japanese that they had to depend upon something other than sheer bravery and capability in combat to overcome our ill-armed troops.

While we, in China, do not expect any powers to fight for us; while we understand their present reluctance to commit themselves to any action likely to be construed as provocative to Japan, there is one thing we do not understand. It is the failure of the powers to try to force Japan to respect those humanitarian principles which are regarded as being the basis of civilization. What governments are reluctant to do, however, peoples can do. They can realistically demonstrate that undeclared warfare, with its revival of barbarism, will not be tolerated. They can assist to bring home to aggressors that no nation that descends to murder, rape, and rapine can expect to prosper or be respected. The Chinese people view with gratitude the steps that have been taken in this regard, and we have profound admiration for the spirit shown by those who have, in no unmistakable voice, made their views and feelings known.

International peace can only come through mutual respect; through mutual observance of treaties, law, and agreements; and through nations collectively acting to discipline anyone that defaults.

We are fighting in China with all our might, as courageously as we can, against formidable odds. Millions of our people are without homes or employment—moving en masse from areas pitilessly ruined by the Japanese—and they do not complain. In one refugee camp the unfortunate inmates went without food for one day so that the cost of that food could be contributed to soldiers at the front to encourage them. All are suffering, or prepared to suffer, and are enduring, and working for victory. We fight because it is our duty to defend our ancient heritage; because it is our hope that justice will come to us, and because it is our belief that the terrible wrongs done in China will yet be righted. We ask only that the people of the democracies will be realistic, will critically examine

Japan's position and actions, and will stand true in upholding the beliefs which they profess and the ethical principles which they espouse. If that is not done the whole world will revert to the days of barbarism, as it has begun in China, and ferocious, unlicensed brutality will be enthroned in those high places where justice, and right, and human decency should hold sway.

13.

MISSIONARIES IN CHINA

"I see a vision of a Chinese Christian Church which can really help China, and enrich Christianity."

SOME years ago it was quite the fashion to decry missionary efforts as being a failure, and I even remember that a commission was sent out from America to gauge the results of missionary work because there was then a widespread feeling that missions had failed in their object. At that time many wondered where were the successors of the Livingstones, the Morrisons, and the Young J. Allens. I think that if one were to view impartially the work done by the missionaries, especially during these months in China, one need no longer doubt whether the same stalwart, courageous, intense passion to help humanity is today present as it was in the days of pioneering missionaries. I may go a step further. I would say, from my personal experience, that almost without a single exception all missionaries who are now in the China field have shown themselves to be possessed of those qualities which we so admired in those missionaries of other days whose names have become famous.

Many people today are thrilled when they read of how Morrison, I think, with a Chinese teacher, worked on his translating the Bible into colloquial, while imperial edicts were sending guards to arrest him. We see something heroic in the way he labored under the uncertain glimmer of an oil lamp risking his life as his sampan traversed tortuous canals so that the masses might have the benefit of the Bible in terms understandable to them.

Today, however, missionaries are working under even greater handicaps of death and woe than those which harassed Morrison. All know only too well what has recently happened in Nanking, Hangchow, Wuhu, and throughout that densely populated region marked by those cities, and how the missionaries have stood their ground and saved hundreds of thousands of our refugees in the face of Japanese bayonets, artillery, bombs, and unbridled lust.

When I was at the front with the Generalissimo I heard stories of women missionaries whose heroism, and whose undaunted resolution to help and work among the stricken people, kept them within the fighting area. There was one woman missionary thirty miles from Hsuchowfu, in a district formerly overrun by bandits, and at that time in daily danger of being entered by the Japanese troops. She was the only foreigner in that district. There was

[298]

another woman, fifty miles north of Hsuchowfu, who, also, was the only foreigner at her station. Then there was a case of two women missionaries going on their way in a sampan. They reached a village where the Chinese troops were destroying all available boats to prevent the Japanese from crossing the Yellow River. Understanding the object of the destruction and sympathizing with our people, these two women voluntarily gave up their sampan to be demolished, one of them remaining to work with the people in that village.

It was the missionaries who foresaw the need of refugee zones, and they established them early in various places. The missionaries in Kaifeng, I understand, are planning a refugee zone on a large, and well-organized scale, in which they expect to take care of thirty thousand women and children should necessity arise. These in Hankow have undertaken the stupendous task of succoring the wounded and the refugees through the International Red Cross.

I could go on enumerating instance after instance of the selflessness and charity of missionary efforts. I need not stress here what missionaries, in the past, have already done in educational, medical, industrial, and agricultural lines to help the people all over the country. It is interesting in passing, however, to mention that when the Generalissimo and I made the first tour of the country, the response of the missionaries everywhere to our request for help in the New Life Movement was tremendous. They felt, and could see, that this movement had unique possibilities of touching the lives of the people and of raising their spiritual and material levels. And so, throughout the country, wherever help has been called for, the missionaries have given themselves wholeheartedly.

How best can the missionaries help us in this national crisis? By continuing their efforts in the same direction in which they have employed them in the past. From the most unexpected sources I have heard admiration of their work. One of our Cabinet Ministers, who is a non-Christian, remarked one day that he was studying the Bible. When asked if he was a Christian, he replied, "No, but I notice that the Christians throughout the country show a greater self-sacrificing spirit than others, and, therefore, I feel that there must be something to Christianity." Another high government official, also a non-Christian, spoke of the spirit to resist and defend the country, which is now prevailing among our masses, as being similar to that spirit of supreme sacrifice that actuated Jesus Christ when he went to Gethsemane to face the Cross.

Some years ago there was much criticism of missionary effort among our Chinese people. Today those who criticized in the past have been completely won over. It is certainly true that actions speak louder than words, and this period of trial and suffering has proved this axiom.

Although the actual work that missionaries have been doing, and are doing, is noteworthy, there is one point which I wish to stress, and that is that the spirit which underlies their ceaseless efforts is recognized as one of the greatest contributions that can be made to our people. By their work and the spirit that underlies it, they have made manifest the meaning of true Christianity. The results of their efforts are so appreciated by the government and the people that the Generalissimo has now found it possible to have that law forbidding religion to be compulsorily taught in Christian schools amended so that religious subjects may henceforth be taught in registered mission schools. This decision is the greatest testimony in the history of China of our appreciation of the value of the real, vital contribution that Christianity has made to the spiritual well-being and the livelihood of our people.

14.

NATIONAL DEFENSE AND
NATIONAL RECONSTRUCTION

*"We must fortify ourselves with the
determination that the greater the obstacles and difficulties the more unflinching and resolute shall be our
resistance."*

I HAVE seen many foreigners, most of them being repre-
sentatives of various governments, or men of affairs, or
newspaper correspondents. Without exception they have
professed great admiration not only for the courage of our
troops, but also because China seems to have achieved
national unity at last.

However, most of them have asked me this question:
"After the war will China still continue to be unified, or
will there be internal dissension? And if there is dissension, what will be the probable effect on the future of our
country?" My answer is: "Yes, there is unity in our

[303]

country now, and, if the sufferings and hardships we have undergone because of this 'undeclared' war have not taught us the necessity and the importance of co-operation, then China deserves to be doomed."

The greatest need of the country, to my mind, is unity and co-operation of all parties and sections of society. It is consequently necessary to devise a national program for all women of China in order that we may correlate the various lines of work which we are doing. For example, in Kiangsi, Hunan, Szechwan, Kwangsi, Chekiang, and elsewhere, we often hear that the women are doing such and such a piece of work, but we do not have definite ideas about it. We are all so-called educated women; at the same time, each one of us is an individual, each with talents, training, convictions, and interests peculiar to herself. It would be folly, therefore, to expect all of us to be as alike as peas, yet we are all members of one body, like hands, arms, legs, and feet; and to obtain the greatest usefulness for that body, there must be correlation of different types of work. So that we may learn from each other the various conditions and problems involved, and the methods used in that work, it is of immense help for us to have firsthand reports from the people who are actually carrying on the work. Also, there is inspiration to be gained from the knowledge of what others are doing.

Let us consider, as the basis of such a program:

(1) How women can serve during the war.
(2) How to mobilize women.
(3) How to encourage productive enterprises by women.
(4) How to improve the livelihood of women.
(5) How best to correlate the work of various women's organizations.

Everyone with whom I have talked has agreed that we must have more trained workers. But there has been some question as to how, and under what auspices, this work is to be carried on in order to ensure lasting success. After much thought I have come to the conclusion that we should use an organization that is already at work, which has national significance, and which can reach the people of all classes and sections of society. I refer to the New Life Movement.

The purpose of the New Life Movement is to help the people, to train them to take their rightful places in society, and to enable them to become useful citizens in a modern democracy.

There are no political purposes attached to the New Life Movement. It is not interested in any way in factional or party maneuvering, nor should it be. I am sure all of us recognize that during this period of our life and death struggle for the survival of our nation, our highest

[305]

duty is to serve only the nation, and disregard personal ambitions and loyalties to lesser causes. This can be accomplished only through unselfish devotion and sacrifice of all of us as individuals.

*   *   *

The task of national defense and reconstruction is the duty of us all. We each have our individual contribution to make, and, it is also true, the nature and scope of our contributions are different. For example, some of us are creative thinkers, some writers, others have professional training, others make their best contributions through spiritual stimulation, while still others secure the best results by actually working in the cities and villages.

We have two hundred million women in this country. How few of our women have had educational opportunities! In view of the fact that the majority of us are not educated, the proportion of educated women seems alarmingly insignificant and ineffective. The two hundred million of our fellow women, however, are like the flour from which bread is made, and we, the educated women, may be likened to the leaven. In order to make the flour into palatable bread the leaven must do the work through being thoroughly mixed with the flour. It is so with us. We must somehow reach the rest of our womanhood.

[306]

I have spoken of what our duty should be toward our country in this crisis, and now as to how we may work in order to get the quickest and most beneficial results:

(1) We must strive, and we must work unceasingly. We must have firm determination and resolute courage to carry on in all circumstances. When we study the history of great nations we see that for a nation to become great, and for a nation to attain independence and equality with other powers, it has to conquer many obstacles and employ unflinching courage in facing realities.

(2) I have mentioned the necessity of unity and co-operation. I wish again to emphasize that if we are to accomplish results we must have selfless devotion to our cause; we must remember that in unity there is strength, that the welfare of the country demands our highest loyalties, and that all other loyalties should be subordinated.

(3) It is essential that there be self-confidence. We must believe that we are capable of building up a new nation, and we must be cheerful in the face of national disasters. If one has courage and foresight, half the battle is already won, because victory depends as much upon the morale of the soldiers and the nation as upon material equipment. There may be some who might say: "Why did we not think of these things before?" It is true that we should have thought of them, and we should have done certain things. However, it is never too late to mend. At

the beginning of the World War, for instance, Great Britain had to depend upon her supplies from her colonies and from other countries. But when the Germans developed their submarine warfare so that it became difficult for Great Britain to get supplies from her usual sources she immediately took steps to increase her own agricultural production. France, too, at the beginning of the World War had no heavy industries to speak of, but that did not deter her from immediately going to work to build up the necessary industries by scientific methods. Speaking of France reminds me that at one time of the war the Germans were within a comparatively few kilometers of Paris, but that in the end it was Germany who lost the war.

We should never forget that, and never despair or give up fighting for our homeland. Let us remember that the Japanese thought that with the withdrawal of our troops from Nanking the war would be over. They thought the same with regard to Hsuchowfu. Yet, today, our armies — in fighting morale, in discipline, in equipment (inadequate as it is), and in knowledge of military tactics — are in a far better position than they were. Our withdrawal from the Capital did not mean that we had lost the war. China, unlike France, has enormous territory, and, if it suits our strategy to withdraw farther inland, we shall withdraw so that the final outcome of the war will be victory for us and for our cause. A good chess player often permits his opponent to take a few pieces in order that he, himself, may win in the end. In time we defeated the Japanese at Taierhchwang — admittedly their first serious military reverse. But I wish to remind each one of you that our Chinese adjuration "not to be proud over victories, not to be downcast over defeats" should be borne in mind all the time.

Let me mention a significant fact. With the exception of Spain and China, which are suffering from calamities caused by the war, all nations are arming and rearming in preparation for a second world war. But we, in China, although involved in an "undeclared" war of aggression that was forced upon us, one that we are going to carry to a finish, are just as actively laying foundations, based on the Three People's Principles, for the reconstruction of a new China when the conflict is ended.

All of us have the deepest admiration for the valor and courage of our men who have made the supreme sacrifice in the defense of our soil. It is, therefore, incumbent upon all of us who are still living not to neglect our supreme duty, which is to continue fighting for the principles for which our heroes have fought and have died. And we need not be ashamed that we are living, for while it is glorious to die for the country it is just as necessary for some of us to live for the country so that we may carry on the unfinished work of those who have given up their lives. We can now do double duty. We have to carry on our own work and we must also carry on the work of those who have died. We must also educate, provide for, and bring up the children they have left behind to be worthy of their fathers.

We are fighting for righteousness, for national existence, and for the survival of our race. The almost incredible heroism of our troops, and the resolute determination of the whole nation to defend ourselves against the Japanese invaders have wiped out all the national humiliation days which have hitherto crowded the calendar in our national history. The whole world now recognizes that we are fighting for righteousness, for not long ago some of our airplanes flew to Japan but did not drop bombs or machine-gun the Japanese civilians, or destroy their homes or businesses. They merely dropped pamphlets to inform and enlighten the Japanese people regarding the cruelties and ruthlessness of the Japanese military. We did not harm the civilians because we have no hatred against the Japanese people. Our country is not at war against those people but against the Japanese militarists who are invading our country, burning our towns and villages, slaughtering our men, raping our women, killing or kidnaping our children, and doing everything they can to annihilate our race, our culture, and our civilization. The Japanese invaders are committing these terrible outrages while they profess to the world that they are only animated by the desire to make "friends" with the Chinese people, to develop economic "co-operation" with them, and to establish "peace" in the Far East. They create war, they thus confess, so that they can create "peace." An amazing proposition. Do they imagine the world is blind? Do they believe that it is populated by fools? Apparently they do — but in their strenuous search for "friendship," for "co-operation," and for "peace," they have compelled our people to suffer unparalleled agonies and humiliations. These hardships have, however, been met and endured in a manner that has astounded the world and evoked its plaudits and its sympathy. Our nation was progressing fast along the highway to organized progress and prosperity when the Japanese violation of our land and our people began. We have, so far, made tremendous sacrifices; met with great difficulties. We shall have to continue meeting those conditions. The road ahead is far from easy. We must face the fact that the immediate future is pregnant with grave happenings which will impose upon us still more intensified sufferings and sacrifices. We have to ask ourselves a clear-cut question: Should we forsake our principles because of the threatening future that these facts envisage? No! Have we the forthright courage to continue fighting for our national existence; for our sovereign rights; for our very lives? Yes! We must fortify ourselves with the determination that the greater the obstacles and difficulties we encounter the more unflinching and resolute should be our resistance. We must continue striving until we have achieved our objective — which is the salvation of our country and the preservation of our ancient heritage.

To give up will mean certain death and destruction. It will mean that all that China has accomplished since our Revolution will be swept away.

Some thirty years ago Dr. Sun Yat-sen said that our people were like a handful of sand, each an individualist. If Dr. Sun were here today I am sure he would be happy to find that since he made that comparison the nation has made wonderful advances toward unity, and that we are now cemented together as we never have been before. Because we are united, and because all sections of society and all parts of the country are working shoulder to shoulder, as exemplified by the magnitude of our national effort against the invading Japanese armies, I am sure the spirit of our great leader must be greatly comforted.

Set in Linotype Estienne type
Format by A. W. Rushmore
Composed and printed by The Golden Eagle Press
Published by HARPER & BROTHERS, New York and London